God and Governing

God and Governing

Reflections on Ethics, Virtue, and Statesmanship

Edited by
ROGER N. OVERTON

☙PICKWICK *Publications* • Eugene, Oregon

GOD AND GOVERNING
Reflections on Ethics, Virtue, and Statesmanship

Copyright © 2009 Wipf and Stock Publishers. All rights reserved. Except for brief quotations in critical publications or reviews, no part of this book may be reproduced in any manner without prior written permission from the publisher. Write: Permissions, Wipf and Stock Publishers, 199 W. 8th Ave., Suite 3, Eugene, OR 97401.

Scripture taken from the New American Standard Bible®, Copyright © 1960,1962, 1963,1968,1971,1972,1973,1975,1977,1995 by The Lockman Foundation. Used by permission.

Pickwick Publications
A Division of Wipf and Stock Publishers
199 W. 8th Ave., Suite 3
Eugene, OR 97401

ISBN 13: 978-1-60608-774-9

Cataloging-in-Publication data:

> God and governing : reflections on ethics, virtue, and statesmanship / edited by Roger N. Overton
>
> xiv + 130 p. ; 23 cm.
>
> ISBN 13: 978-1-60608-774-9
>
> 1. Christianity and politics—United States. 2. Evangelicalism—Political aspects—United States. I. Overton, Roger N. II. Title.

R516 G55 2009

Manufactured in the U.S.A.

In honor of

Margaret Holtrust, John Holtrust, and the Holtrust family

Contents

Foreword by Charles Colson / ix

Introduction *by Roger N. Overton* / 1

1 Why Being Good Is So Political *by David F. Wells* / 7

2 The Travails of Evangelical Politics *by Paul Marshall* / 28

3 The Golden Triangle of Freedom *by Os Guinness* / 41

4 Lessons on Fleeing Temptation *by Patrick Nolan* / 50

5 The Future of Virtue and Statesmanship in Pagan America *by Vishal Mangalwadi* / 62

6 The Failure of Evangelical Political Involvement *by Dallas Willard* / 74

7 Practical Ways Forward *by Donald McConnell* / 92

8 Justice in Evangelical Political Theology *by Stephen Kennedy* / 108

List of Contributors / 127

Foreword

TEN YEARS AGO, THE late Paul Weyrich created a major stir when he told cultural conservatives that "we probably have lost the culture war." He advised his followers "to drop out of this culture, and find places where we can live godly, righteous and sober lives."

While I respected Weyrich, I thought he was absolutely wrong. When great culture wars are raging, Christians have no business fleeing the field of battle. There is a proper, biblically-mandated role for us to play in public life.

This lesson was taught to us some two hundred years ago by a man who is a role model for my life: William Wilberforce, the great British abolitionist, member of parliament, and a Christian. When Wilberforce began what he called his "two great objects"—the abolition of the slave trade and the "reformation of manners"—his circumstances could not have been more daunting. England's economy was heavily dependent upon the slave trade. The prospect of reforming manners, or "morals" as we would say today, was no less daunting. Public drunkenness and crime were rampant. The elites of Wilberforce's day, like those of our own, were contemptuous of morality. In fact, it was fashionable among the landed gentry to be loose in morals and skeptical about religion.

Yet, fifty years after Wilberforce began his twin crusades, this had all been turned around. Slavery was abolished in the British Empire. Piety and virtue went from being despised to being fashionable.

This remarkable turnaround would not have happened if Wilberforce had allowed the inevitable setbacks of any great struggle to cause him to quit. In fact, for twenty years he fought every year in parliament and was voted down, until the slave trade was finally abolished in 1807.

Wilberforce's life should serve as an example for all of us, and a reminder that God calls us to engage in all of life, including politics. And, as Roger Overton notes in the introduction to this book, Christians who live in countries based on democratic principles hold a special privilege and responsibility to influence their society through political involvement, rooted in our mandate to be a blessing to our neighbors.

The doctrine of creation tells us the state is ordained by God; therefore, participation in political life is a moral obligation, contained in the cultural mandate to cultivate the world God created. We should seek justice and order in political structures, striving to be the best of citizens, as Augustine put it, because we do for love of God what others do only because they are coerced by law.

And yet, because the state is not the only social institution ordained by God, we must work to keep its scope limited, or we may run the risk of succumbing to what Jacques Ellul, the eccentric French Reformed thinker, prophesied in the 1960s: the politicization of all aspects of life—the idea that every problem has a political solution. This, Ellul warned, leads to increasing dependence on the state by ordinary citizens and decreasing citizen control of government. Programs will pile upon programs, agencies upon agencies, until the whole structure of government becomes so unwieldy it can hardly function. We saw this happen in the wake of Hurricane Katrina, and I fear we might see it again during another terrorist attack.

Just as Paul Weyrich and others who counsel withdrawal from the public square are, I believe, in error, so too are those who miss the mark on the other side—seeing politics as the ultimate authority. Even Christians can succumb to the political illusion. Several years ago, a Christian leader blurted, "I think we have been legislated out of the possibility of a spiritual revival." Some Christians seem almost defeatist when "our" candidate loses. But the real evil of the illusion is that it distracts us from other aspects of life. We must keep political activity in perspective, seeing that it fulfills its proper role, in what Dutch politician and church leader Abraham Kuyper and other reformers called "sphere sovereignty"—each sphere (family, church, government) carrying out its own responsibility before God.

Even then, we must take great care in how we go about achieving political goals. During the aftermath of *Roe v. Wade*, when evangelicals assumed a much greater role in politics, there was a tendency to believe that the best way to achieve political goals was to align with a political party. But Christians should never muddy the revealed truth of the gospel with political ideology; the gospel is never to be held hostage to any partisan agenda.

Foreword

If we allow this to happen, politicians and the media will treat us as just another special interest group to be placated. But we Christians do not (or should not) ask Republicans or Democrats to adopt our agenda because we constitute a powerful special-interest group, like labor unions. We don't support any party in order to achieve political gains; we ask for pro-family and pro-life policies from both political parties because these policies are right for our country. Even if evangelicals did not cast one single vote for the party in power, we would still vigorously insist that its leaders support biblically-informed policies.

Christians, remember, are the guardians of the 3,000-year-old moral tradition—largely influenced by Judeo-Christian revelation—that has nurtured Western civilization. That is why we speak out on behalf of these traditional human values. Think about what is most praiseworthy about life in America: respect for the person, and beliefs about liberty and justice. These ideas had their origins in the biblical revelation. Christians engage in the political process to remind the culture and politicians alike about the work our leaders should be about. We do so because, in recent decades, government policies have ignored the most cherished values of our heritage. Liberty has been turned into licentiousness.

Like our evangelical forebears who spent decades fighting against slavery in America, we modern Christians involve ourselves in politics not to gain power, but to get politicians to do what they ought to do because it is right—because it conforms to the moral order by which we live as a civilized people.

As we do so, we should take another lesson from Wilberforce. His long and frustrating battle against the slave trade did not turn him into a dour scold. In fact, one of his contemporaries called him "the most amusable man I've ever known." That is, he was amiable and enjoyed even the company of those with whom he disagreed. As Donald McConnell notes in ch. 7, Christians should plunge into the political realm with a strong commitment to civility.

Finally, as Stephen Kennedy indicates in ch. 8, Christians must not enter the public square armed with nothing more than religious clichés for arguments. "The Bible says so" is not typically convincing. We must learn to make prudential arguments for the policies we promote. For example, Prison Fellowship is dedicated to what we call restorative justice—a concept based on biblical principle. Rather than simply seeking retribution for crime and building more prisons, restorative justice holds that we should work to restore lawbreakers into their communities as changed and productive members of society. We should also help the victims of crime, restoring what the Jews called the *shalom* of the community.

We do not simply say we urge and do this because the Bible teaches it; rather, we take our position on prudential grounds. It is the best policy. When we do this, we often can witness to our faith in a more winsome manner. For example, I have visited state legislatures all over America to speak about restitution. I tell them, "Instead of locking up non-violent offenders in cells that cost the taxpayers $30,000 a year, make them work and pay back their victims." Lawmakers come up to me afterwards and say, "That's a great idea, Mr. Colson. Where did it come from?" I say to them, "Have you got a Bible at home? Dust it off. Restorative justice is a concept out of the Old Testament."

The prospect of turning around our culture may seem overwhelming at times. But withdrawal from the fray is inconsistent with loving our neighbor—whether that neighbor is an unborn child or the abortionist who tries to take the child's life. Bible-believing Christians have achieved great political successes throughout history: religious freedom, abolition, civil rights. In recent years, we have fought pitched battles against pornography and the trafficking of women and children, for human rights in Darfur and North Korea, and against the destruction of marriage here at home.

The most praiseworthy elements of American life have their origins in the biblical tradition. Christianity has played a tremendous role throughout history in preserving political freedom in the West, and Christian values are needed to sustain them today. Our faith gives us the perspective to define our purposes, not by the standards of the world, but according to God's purposes.

This understanding is a source of courage as we continue to fight the battles for righteousness begun by earlier generations of Christians—even when the odds are stacked heavily against us. The contributors in this book will help readers gain a greater understanding of why evangelicals cannot, *must* not, drop out of the public square, and how to go about redeeming the culture in a godly way.

Because we live in a fallen world, we must be realistic about the limits of political success. Our accomplishments will always be partial, temporary, and painfully inadequate. There is no room for the excessive triumphalism we saw during the rise of the Religious Right. Nevertheless,

Foreword

we must not choose between living godly, righteous lives, as Paul Weyrich suggested, and participating in redeeming the culture through politics. For our neighbor's sakes, as well as for God's, we are called to do both.

Charles Colson

Introduction

> For surely organized Christianity presupposes civilization. It is preached and practiced effectively within an ordered polity.[1]
>
> —Harry Blamires

AT THE CENTER OF the Christian faith is the God-man, the Christ. He is the image of the all-powerful creator of the universe, born in human flesh in an Israeli back alley. All Christian hope is placed in him, in what he accomplished through death by Roman execution and in what lies ahead when he finally returns with a two-edged sword. As powerful as this message is, there is a sense in which the spreading of this message depends on a certain amount of social order. Theologian Harry Blamires explains, "In a jungle, where cannibals dine on missionary stew, where men prey bestially upon another, certain preliminary steps toward minimal restraint, hygiene, and the guarantee of continuing survival have to be taken before a prayer meeting can be arranged and the gospel proclaimed."[2] There must be some level of common civility in order for the love of Christ to be demonstrated and good news of his work explained, and this common civility often comes through political social order.

Even Christ depended on such an atmosphere. "Our Lord's work was done within a province of the Roman Empire where the appurtenances and safe-guards of civilized life were available. He was able to read, to argue in the temple, and, in his teaching, to use allusions and references that implied a residuum of knowledge in his hearers derived from their own culture and tradition."[3] Thus, Christians throughout history have found themselves in a world directed by some degree of politic. Through eras

---

1. Harry Blamires, *Where Do We Stand? A Christian Response to Secularism* (Vancouver, BC: Regent College Publishing, 2006), 17.
2. Ibid, 17.
3. Ibid, 18.

of social persecution, tolerance, acceptance and dominance, Christians have sought to understand just how their faith should interact with the political environment in which they find themselves.

The political foundations of the United States of America provide an environment practically unparalleled in human history, primarily due to "freedom of religion." In America, there is principally no state sponsored religion or religion sponsored state, nor is there discrimination against most varieties of religious beliefs. A diversity of faiths have found America to be a safe haven for belief and practice, whether they seclude themselves from the general public or take office in the highest levels of government. Religious believers not only have the opportunity to exist peacefully, but also to participate in the policies and actions of the government. It may well be argued that Christians have not only the privilege, but also the responsibility, to affect their society through political action. The crux of the argument rests on the commandment to "love thy neighbor." Certainly the commandment primarily has in mind caring for others' eternal salvation through preaching the gospel and sacrificial giving, but love can also take the form of seeking social policy that will be of benefit to one's neighbor. Many people have found, however, that there are grave dangers in taking this concept too far.

In 1979, a political action group called the Moral Majority was founded by evangelist Jerry Falwell. The group, which claimed to be nonpartisan, sought the promotion of morality in culture, and, by extension, sought the failure of whatever legislation it deemed immoral. The group had a platform centering on commitment to separation of church and state, life, and traditional family; support for Jews and Israel, a strong national defense, equal rights for women, and the freedom of state organizations to act apart from federal control; and opposition to illegal drug trafficking, pornography, and the Equal Rights Amendment. Though the Religious Right movement was already forming prior to the advent of the Moral Majority, the action group became the most potent force for religious conservative power. Many analysts credited the group with helping Ronald Reagan defeat Jimmy Carter in the 1980 presidential election. Falwell dissolved the group in 1989, though much of its work continued with the newly founded Christian Coalition. For good or for ill, conservative Christians have been associated with these groups in the public mind ever since.

Introduction

As key members of the Moral Majority, Cal Thomas and Ed Dobson published the book *Blinded by Might*, reflecting on the successes and failures of the group.[4] Dobson notes that the Moral Majority was not a complete waste of time and money. It brought moral and religious issues to the forefront of public discussion and called Christians to civic responsibility by the millions. But the bulk of the book seeks to explain why the group's goals were largely wrongheaded. Dobson explains, "We failed not because we were wrong about our critique of culture, or because we lacked conviction, or because there were not enough of us, or because too many were lethargic and uncommitted. We failed because we were unable to redirect a nation from the top down."[5] The danger in seeking to "love thy neighbor" primarily through political means is that Christians can come to trust in the political system more than in the work and power of the Christ to change hearts and lives. Cal Thomas puts it this way: "Most children learn after unsuccessful attempts to fit a square peg in a round hole that it isn't going to work . . . It appears that too many religious conservatives have not learned from twenty years of attempts to fit the square peg of the kingdom not of this world into the round hole that is the kingdom of this world."[6]

Just in case it's not obvious, very little of what the Religious Right has fought so hard for over these past three decades has changed. Abortion and same-sex marriage still divide America, while indecent television programming and pornography are more pervasive than ever. Some on the Religious Right will claim that now, under President Barack Obama, they have in fact lost ground. As this book is being sent to press, federal restrictions against embryonic stem cell research are being struck down and there are plans to suspend protections for doctors who refuse to perform abortions. How is it that after so much time, money, campaigning, and political gusto, evangelicals on both the left and the right have failed to make any sort of significant impact on the political landscape? In February of 2008, Trinity Law School gathered some of the brightest minds in evangelical theological and political thought for a "God and Governing" conference to reflect on the question of what went wrong.

---

4. Cal Thomas and Ed Dobson, *Blinded by Might: Can the Religious Right Save America?* (Grand Rapids, Michigan: Zondervan, 1999), 43.

5. Ibid, 23.

6. Ibid, 139.

With the exception of one lecture, all of the presentations from the conference are represented in this book for a wider audience.[7]

David Wells begins the book by reflecting on the common view that Christianity is nothing more than a political action group. He claims that evangelicals "have thought thoughts that were too small, too partisan, too fragmented, and too muddled and they therefore are in danger of losing their way." America grew up within the moral framework of freedom and equality, which was sustained by the domain of "obedience to the unenforceable." Wells provides historical background to explain how culture's authority shifted from moral norms to an ever-expanding government, and how evangelicals now also tend to look to the government to solve society's problems. He argues that our task is to refocus Christian activism toward the cultivation of virtuous character as a means for changing the political landscape. In chapter 2, Paul Marshall addresses the problems of shallow political thought, inappropriate biblicism, misguided activism, and the overestimation of prophecy. Marshall argues that these problems result in a lack of any robust Christian political theory that can be applied throughout the various political situations facing people across the globe today. Fortunately, there are select Christians involved in real politic struggles who can model the union of a thorough Christian worldview with a thoughtful and effective political life.

Freedom is not free, nor is it often even understood correctly. The third chapter, written by Os Guinness, explores the foundations of freedom in the American political system and the cultural shifts that have warped the modern concept of freedom. Guinness exposes the common menaces opposed to freedom and challenges the current generation to take responsibility and sustain freedom in coming years.

Patrick Nolan, once the most powerful Republican leader in California's legislature, recounts in chapter 4 how he ended up in prison convicted of corruption and how this changed his life. Told by a friend to view his time in prison as a monastic experience, Nolan says, "I went into prison believing in God and came out knowing Him." Nolan reflects on the many temptations that confront leaders in government and business, and provides practical ways Christians can be alert to temptations and stay on the right path.

---

7. The second lecture by Os Guinness is based on his book *The Case for Civility: And Why Our Future Depends on It* (New York: HarperOne, 2008). We commend the book to readers who have further interest in the issues discussed here.

Introduction

Relativism and destructive views of sexuality are some of the reasons Vishal Mangalwadi believes America is becoming increasingly pagan. In chapter 5, he retraces similar problems he encountered while he lived and ministered with his wife in India, warning that unless immediate changes are made to America's present course, it will end up the same way.

Dallas Willard argues in chapter 6 that there seems to be little or no improvement in the ethical quality of American political discourse, because of three major factors: There is a lack of connection between the evangelical "gospel" and character development; moral knowledge has disappeared from the "institutions of knowledge" in our society; and, there has been a general withering of professional ethos, such that a professional's life is no longer tied to an exalted vision of dignity and the public good. To recover ethical maturity in political discourse, Willard argues, evangelical leaders must lead the charge by arguing for biblical truths as knowledge of reality. They must proclaim, defend, and practice those truths as known by themselves and available to others as knowledge.

Donald McConnell, dean of Trinity Law School, points out nine practical ways forward for evangelicals in chapter 7. These include recognizing human fallibility, committing to objective truth and morality, connecting right doctrine with right living, and standing for freedom within the rule of law. He concludes with a call for Christians to pursue careers in law and politics. Concluding the book is a chapter by Stephen Kennedy reflecting on the role of justice in Christian political duty. Kennedy explores the implications of creation and the Trinity for how Christians ought to act within a national community. He argues that every right is reciprocated by a duty and that our existence in sociable community is a reflection of God existing eternally in three persons. Understanding the implications of these concepts with a commitment to virtue will help Christians engage and shape the culture in positive ways.

As was mentioned earlier, the "God and Governing" conference was orchestrated by Trinity Law School, so this book would not have come to fruition without the guidance of Dean McConnell and many volunteers, many of whom sacrificed more than just a weekend to make the conference happen. Among them was Christopher Neiswonger, one of the great minds behind Apologetics.com. Our gratitude is also due to Charles Colson for seeing the value of this project and contributing the foreword. I am personally grateful to California Assemblyman Chuck DeVore for the many suggestions he offered to improve the book. Finally, we would like to thank Diane Farley, our editor Christopher Spinks, and the rest of the staff at Wipf & Stock, for their careful help in bringing this book to print.

Trinity Law School is on a mission to make a difference in the world through biblically-minded legal education. As McConnell points out in his chapter, there is a great need for biblically-minded Christians to pursue careers in law and politics. The law school is at the top of the class in training Christians with a theologically and ethically integrated worldview that addresses every facet of law and government from a deeply biblical perspective. Those interested in finding out more about Trinity Law School should visit their website, www.tiu.edu.

Roger Overton
April 2009

1

Why Being Good Is So Political

David F. Wells

INTRODUCTION

THAT EVANGELICALS VOTED ON opposite sides in the 2008 presidential election which brought Obama to the White House, and that they evaluated the issues at stake differently, is rather clear. While it is inevitable that some differences will always be evident in the way that Christians think, how we think should never be narrowly partisan. There are, so to speak, much larger fish that need to be fried. That is what I want to consider in this essay.

In fact, the argument I want to advance is that evangelicals have not distinguished themselves in recent engagements with political issues. It is not because they thought thoughts that were too bold about the ordering of America's political and social life, thoughts that were too adventurous, or too big, and then failed. Rather, they have often failed because they have thought thoughts that were too small, too partisan, too fragmented, and too muddled, and they are therefore in danger of losing their way.

There is a difference between politics and culture, but today this difference is often obscured and this works itself out in the assumption that the right political program will also right our social life, as well as many of our social wrongs. Some of the more politically vocal evangelicals, therefore, have pursued political issues with a new intensity in recent decades in step with their perception that America is sliding into moral decay. Their hope seems to have been that by this political involvement, America will be transformed.

The problem, of course, is that exposed to the vagaries of competing political agendas, they find themselves, as sociologist David Martin says, "with little more than native good sense and the limited inferences they can draw from the Bible."[1] But they also find themselves, despite the biblical truth they hold, with a diminished understanding of corrupted human nature, exaggerated expectations about what the political process can accomplish, and confusion about how best to address issues that are more cultural than political, more about human nature than about government policy. So, let us begin by thinking about the place of morality in our public life.

MORAL FRAMING

American democracy, like other modern democracies, is liberal in the sense that it is, on principle, both inclusive and impartial. It is inclusive in that all its people are *citizens* rather than subjects. It is impartial in that all its citizens have equal standing before the law, equal weight within the electoral processes, and an equal right to believe whatever they want to believe.[2] It is, of course, this last point that makes democracies vulnerable because all democracies are as strong or as frail as the people who exercise their right to believe whatever it is that they want to believe. Government may be representative but, as Alexis de Tocqueville observed long ago, it is also "clear that the opinions, prejudices, interests, and even passions of the people can find no lasting obstacles preventing them from being manifest in the daily conduct of society."[3] It is true, as James Madison observed, that government would not be necessary if all people were angelic. But it is just as true, as Madison also recognized, that government has only a limited capacity to restrain fallen passions. The founders of the American democracy never imagined that the government had the power to restrain many of the human passions. These passions would have to be restrained by religion and morality if the Constitution was to work.[4]

---

1. David Martin, "The Evangelical Upsurge and Its Political Implications," in *The Desecularization of the World: Resurgent Religion and World Politics*, edited by Peter L. Berger (Grand Rapids: Eerdmans, 1999), 39.

2. Nicholas Woltersdorff, "The Role of Religion in Political Issues," in *Religion in the Public Square: The Place of Religious Convictions in Political Debate*, edited by Robert Audi and Nicholas Wolterstorff (New York: Rowman and Littlefield, 1997), 69-72.

3. Alexis de Tocqueville, *Democracy in America*, edited by J. P. Mayer, translated by George Lawrence (2 vols.; New York: Harper & Row, 1969), 1:173.

4. Cf; the comments by Malcolm Muggeridge: "No people, it is safe to say, in all his-

Why Being Good Is So Political

This, then, was the basis on which Tocqueville went on to contrast political parties that are "great" from those that are not. In the former category are those parties that are fundamentally about *principles* rather than consequences, about *ideas* rather than personalities. They seek to articulate national priorities in terms of a Good that trumps all individual passions and prejudices. They are great because they are able to harness the opinions and interests of a majority in realizing ends that are greater then mere private interest. This means that all are asked, in some measure, to subjugate some aspect of self-interest, but it is important to remember that this kind of self-subjugation produces no enduring long-term national redemption. It remains a condition of national flourishing that must be constantly renewed.

Unless demands are made on all, and made out of moral considerations and not just political calculation, we are left to live in the solitude of our own internal worlds amidst the clashing interests of private, unregulated passions. Lofty convictions stir people beyond their private worlds and private interests whereas the base agendas of the "small parties," are only about petty self-interest. They corrupt society. As the great ideas about society disintegrate, ironic as it is, people are left happier, but the nation is left less moral, Tocqueville asserted.[5]

So what is it, we should be asking ourselves, that makes for a healthy democracy, one that is about great ideas? It is, at the very least, that kind of democracy which is seeking the common Good—which, if it is truly good, is necessarily moral in its nature. Democracy, as Aristotle observed a long time ago, is about people freely deliberating together on how they ought to order their common life. If we are serious about this language of

---

tory have been so specifically and lavishly certified to be free and in the full enjoyment of all their human rights as the Americans. Yet, I asked myself, were their human rights real or illusionary? Certainly, as long as they had money, unlike the Muscovites, they could do as they pleased, read whatever they wanted to read, go wherever they had a mind to. Moreover, thanks to the Supreme Court and other judiciaries, their human rights were constantly being extended, so that they could sleep with whomever they wanted to sleep with, male or female, break a marriage and enter into another just as the fancy took them, choose any one of an increasing variety of television programs, abort an inconvenient birth, stupefy themselves with drugs, immerse themselves in porn, and ultimately, if they so wished, just with the aid of a hypodermic syringe or some sleeping tablets, bring their days to an end . . . Was it freedom ever burgeoning or a servitude ever more exacting?" Malcolm Muggeridge, "Human and Divine Rights," in *At the Edge of Hope: Christian Laity in Paradox*, edited by Howard Butt (New York: Seabury, 1978), 61.

5. Tocqueville, *Democracy in America*, 1:175.

ought then we are saying that public life is to be framed and directed by moral considerations. These considerations should trump private interest, which is often carried out in all the new forms of tribalism that are coalescing. Western forms of tribalism are not simply ethnic. Rather, what has emerged are coalitions centered on an interest the coalition has in common. It is a *self*-interest that is being realized in the group's interest. Its service feeds those whose interest it is, usually at the expense of others. Among these new tribes are the generational clusters—the Builders, Boomers, Gen-Xers, and Millennials; gender preoccupations, which seek to draw those of the same gender into coalition; and, of course, the old racial interests, which divide the political landscape along racial lines. Religious tribes also mark our national discussion. Political life, cultural critic Craig Gay writes, is "a kind of window into the soul of a people, revealing their most basic assumptions about the nature of the world and their most cherished aspirations for life within it."[6] And some of those most basic assumptions have to do with this tribal consciousness in our postmodern forms.

The question that has to be answered, then, concerns how those most basic and cherished aspirations about life are going to be realized and how they are going to be disciplined. And here we have a clear fork in the road. We have to distinguish between habits of the heart that, through the political process, can be given public shape, and those habits of the heart that need to be disciplined by means other than the political process. Habits of the heart may be for good or ill, and this raises the most basic of questions in the life of a democracy. We have to decide how what is good will be played out publicly, and how what is bad will be restrained.

OBEDIENCE TO THE UNENFORCEABLE

A pluralistic society such as ours balks at the idea that any one system of ethics should be given a formal, preferential role in ordering the nation's life, but at the same time, it is worth remembering that both civil and criminal law have already ensconced some moral norms in our national life. Our society is already agreed that it is wrong to murder, rob, rape, slander, and defraud. These actions have been criminalized and they are penalized. Yet the range of moral issues that can be handled through the

---

6. Craig Gay, *The Way of the (Modern) World: Or, Why It's Tempting to Live as If God Doesn't Exist* (Grand Rapids: Eerdmans, 1998), 30.

courts in this way is really quite small and, in any case, the penal code is quite inadequate to provide the moral guidance for much of what happens in our society each day.

The Three Domains

In an illuminating observation, the English jurist John Fletcher Moulton noted that in a democracy such as ours, three domains have to be preserved. On the one side, we have to preserve the domain of law, both criminal and civil, because every society needs this system of restraints against dangerous and harmful human behavior. On the other side, lies the domain of freedom which sustains life in other but equally important ways. It is in this soil that artistic life flourishes, as does capitalism itself, as well as all forms of religious believing including Christian faith.

However, this view of freedom needs to be qualified in important ways. It is quite true that if America is to be true to itself, this freedom needs to be protected. At the same time, it is a freedom that often needs to be restrained for moral reasons. It is a freedom that is not absolute and unqualified. Hence the importance of the third domain.

Lying between law and freedom, then, is this other domain. It is what is characterized, John Fletcher Moulton said, by "obedience to the unenforceable."[7] It is this domain that, in fact, is rooted in the moral fabric of reality. Here restraint comes from within, not from without through the law, be it civil or criminal. It comes from self-discipline, from commitment to a Good that trumps mere self-interest, from the willingness to sacrifice self-interest and self-desire in order to do what is right. And here this decision to act upon what is good, and to avoid what is unethical, is likewise not commanded from without but compelled from within. In the context of Christian faith, of course, this Good is personal and is none other than the triune God of Scripture. Yet even outside of a redemptive context such as this, there is a Good written into the fabric of human nature, which reflects who we are in the image of a moral God (Rom 1:18–20; 2:14–16).

This third domain is quite as important as the other two. After all, most lying is not illegal, but it is always unethical. Selfishness is wrong, from an ethical point of view, but it is not illegal unless it crosses legal lines. Racist attitudes are ethically wrong, but not illegal until they are acted upon. And,

---

7. John Fletcher Moulton, "Law and Manners," *The Atlantic*, July 1924.

on the other side of the coin, while the law can forbid many things that are wrong, it cannot command many things that are right (except by implication). It can forbid assault, but it cannot command kindness and compassion. It can forbid theft, but it cannot command generosity, philanthropy, or care for the abandoned and dispossessed. These are the fruit of ethical and religious commitment. They are born of a sense of moral obligation. They arise from the middle territory, the land of "obedience to the unenforceable," and without this land, a nation is dangerously impoverished. More than that, without this domain, the domains freedom on the one side and law on the other are likely to run amok.

The Lost Domain

So, what happens when, as Barna reported in 2005, only 16 percent of Americans base moral decisions on the content of the Bible? And what happens when 65 percent think that there are no moral absolutes?[8] What happens is that the domain of the "obedience to the unenforceable" begins to disappear, to be held down "in unrighteousness." As this land, as it were, shrinks, law from the one side, and freedom from the other, rush in to occupy its vacated space. The result is that we increasingly look to our nation's laws to regulate behavior, which, in fact, is the proper function of morality. And because America has 70 percent of the world's lawyers, the consequence is that the fear of litigation is often far more persuasive in changing behavior than an appeal to any moral principle. It is one thing for a country's laws to have become derelict and unenforceable. It is quite another to have a situation, such as ours in America, where all that we have is lawyers.

At the same time, though, while law is attempting to encroach on what has been moral turf, so too is freedom. In the absence of a moral framework, freedom is then construed in libertine ways. That is, postmoderns now believe that they are free to see, say, and do anything they want with the sole proviso that it is not illegal. Freedom ends only where the line of illegality begins.

So it is that today, as the domain of "obedience to the unenforceable" disappears, we are caught in this double rip-tide. One threatens to elimi-

---

8. The Barna Group, "Most Adults Feel Accepted by God, but Lack a Biblical Worldview," *Barna Update*, August 9, 2005, n.p., online: http://www.barna.org/barna-update/article/5-barna-update/174-most-adults-feel-accepted-by-god-but-lack-a-biblical-worldview.

nate all genuine freedom by its legal reach into aspects of life in which law and government are blunt, ineffective, and inappropriate instruments while the other threatens to eliminate any role morality might genuinely have in national life because postmoderns want to be free from all moral norms which originate from outside of themselves.

FREEDOM AND EQUALITY

Understanding this dynamic is really the key to understanding much that has happened in American political life, because this political life has taken place within a culture that is particular, in some ways, to America. Here, the most basic of all cultural commitments are those to freedom and equality, so we need to think a little further about this.

Can We Be Both Free and Equal?

In the nineteenth century, Europeans and Americans thought about these concepts differently. In America, freedom came to mean being able to believe what you want, to express those views, and to be able to act on them, provided that action was within the law. Equality came to mean having the same status under the law, the same weight within the electoral processes, and the same unfettered ability to access opportunity without being handicapped by birth, family lines, or socio-economic standing. Europeans believed that these two concepts were inherently opposed to one another. After all, no two people enter life with the same talents, drives, and dispositions and so, as life unfolds and as people are able to exploit their opportunities, some are able to acquire great wealth and to bring about great attainments, but others are not. It is freedom that in the end guarantees that there will be great inequalities. Europeans, therefore, thought that freedom and equality were inherently contradictory.

Americans did not. Americans, Tocqueville observed, were entirely comfortable with the idea that different people would have different attainments in life as well as different accumulations of wealth.[9] This was no violation of equality. What they objected to deeply was the thought that some could not attempt to attain or acquire, that there might be those to whom opportunity would not be allowed to beckon, at least not in the same way as to others because of birth, family lines, or social location. It was equality that allowed freedom to flourish and

---

9. Tocqueville, *Democracy in America*, 1:54.

freedom therefore needed equality if it was to do so. That has been the American view.

The Impulse of Freedom

As it turns out, these twin pillars in the American character—freedom and equality—have produced two strands in our political life that continue to reverberate in each successive presidential election. The commitment to freedom has, in both the liberal and libertarian political traditions, also morphed sometimes into an exaggerated focus on the individual and, in its postmodern incarnation, into an embrace of the autonomous self. "The individual's right to define and pursue (within limits) his own happiness, his own good, his own set of values,"[10] has become paramount, Douglas MacLean and Claudia Mills say. The result is that this kind of political impulse demands that the state protect a sphere within which privacy rights are secured—not least those, for example, having to do with abortion. This is a demand that reads the Constitution in a particular way, but it also goes hand in hand with moral relativism, or it sees the individual's self-interest as itself being a moral norm, or it has an interest in limiting the state's encroachment and reach into private life.

The Impulse of Equality

The other strand, having to do with the basic commitment to equality, has led to the insistence on the part of some that the state attempt to ensure relative parity of wealth by means of taxation so that the rich get richer at a slower rate than the poor get richer. This has been the appeal of many populist crusades, whether Democratic or Republican. If the impulse for freedom has sometimes morphed into that of extreme individualism, that of equality has sometimes morphed into an artificial kind of conformity. Fairness, it comes to be thought, demands that there be a parity in the things possessed, too. A parity reached, if necessary, by a redistribution of wealth through taxation.[11]

---

10. Douglas MacLean and Claudia Mills, editors, *Liberalism Reconsidered* (New Jersey: Rowman and Allanheld, 1983), x.

11. This expectation about being able to participate in the post-War affluence was really fueled by the fact that so many had benefited so that it became a matter of grievance among those who had not. These are the waters in which ambitious politicians have trolled. See Robert N. Bellah et al., *The Good Society* (New York: Knopf, 1991), 52–81.

It was rather clear in the run up to the 2008 presidential election that these two competing impulses defined the way the election issues were framed. On the one side, was this understanding of freedom, on the other this understanding of equality. The Democratic agenda, as the Obama presidency begins, is to offer tax cuts to 95 percent of Americans but to increase the tax burden on the taxpayers who are already paying the lion's share of the tax bill.

These impulses, one keying off the belief in freedom and other off the belief in equality, have the capacity to become socially disruptive if they are not restrained by moral norms outside the political process. Indeed, freedom and equality mean something entirely different depending on whether they are thought about in a moral context or only in a political context. When disconnected from objective moral norms, they become diminished, emasculated, and even damaging impulses. What seems to have spared our country from its moment of reckoning, at least on the side of equality, is that the economy overall has kept expanding or, at least, that we have been able to keep borrowing, and this has propped up our ability to sustain entitlements and large government handouts made for compassionate purposes. It is thus that our national economic demise has been staved off while the promise of equality has been kept alive.

However, there has been a staggering price to pay for this ambitious pursuit. Our borrowing had elevated our collective national debt to $8.68 trillion by the end of 2006, which works out to about $29,000 per person.[12] However, troubling as this is, it looks like the essence of restraint when compared to the final two Bush years and the plans announced by Obama as he began his presidency in 2009. Congress approved a bailout package and stimulus for the economy of $787 billion, which works out to $2,600 per person. The whole rescue package combined will add somewhere in the region of $3 trillion to the national debt, which had ballooned by beginning of 2009 to $13 trillion, with no end in sight.

How will this staggering debt be paid off? There are only two possibilities. Since our history of paying off our national debt is so poor, it is

12. This lavish borrowing was needed, Christopher Lasch has argued, if the country was to satisfy two political objectives that are simply incompatible: that demanded by the right to live off one's property or labor and that demanded by the goal of equality. See Christopher Lasch, "Liberalism in Retreat," in *Liberalism Reconsidered*, edited by Douglas MacLean and Claudia Mills (Totowa, NJ: Rowman & Littlefield, 1983) 105–6. On the themes of Lasch's thought, see Patrick J. Deneen, "Christopher Lasch and the Limits of Hope," *First Things*, December 2004, 26–30.

rather clear that it is very unlikely a debt so large can be paid off merely by raising taxes, especially as raising taxes will stifle the economy and, in turn, reduce revenues that might have gone toward the debt. Therefore, we will either borrow the money or we will print it. If the former, then the debt will be paid by our children and grandchildren. That amounts to generational theft. If the latter, we will all pay it by way of inflation on a level that could become crippling. Those on fixed incomes, the elderly, will be hurt the most. So, who do we want to bear the damage from what we are doing—our children or our elderly?

These economic questions are undoubtedly very complex, and honest people in both parties can legitimately reach different conclusions. However, at least one-third of the stimulus package, and perhaps much more, can only be seen as a payoff to special interests and political constituencies of the Democratic party. It represents items that have long been on the Democrats' shopping list, and the emergency in the country was seized upon as a pretext to do the spending that some have been yearning to do for years. The problem with this is that they had to weigh the political benefits of doing this against the moral costs of asking the young or the elderly to pay the costs for it. They chose the immediate political benefits. They set aside the moral issues. This collective selfishness, this unwillingness to curb our own appetites and this expectation for others later to pay for our current self-indulgence, is simply reprehensible, and both political parties have engaged in it.

WHY WE HAVE FAILED

The role of Christian faith in society is to ask for what is right, to do what is good, and to act, wherever possible, as a restraint on what is morally harmful. This restraint, in almost all cases, is not exercised through law enforcement, necessary as that is, but through influence and persuasion which arises out of the domain of "obedience to the unenforceable." This is where the preservatives of Christian moral character originate, and it is from thence that they come to intersect with a nation's public and social life. It is off this public and social life that politics key.

Political life, though, follows and reflects cultural life. It is not the other way around. Political action and social policies by themselves are only marginally effective in changing the underlying cultural life. The question about the place of evangelicals in the political process, therefore, is more basically a question about their role and their effectiveness in shaping or, at least, affecting the nation's cultural life. It is entirely possible for groups to be highly effective in advocating, and seeing implemented, their political goals while the culture nevertheless moves on somewhat untouched by all of these political moves.

Culture

By *culture* I am thinking not about the older associations with "high culture"; I am thinking in terms that are more sociological than aesthetic. The word *culture* is what describes how the nation's most basic, fundamental understandings about life are encountered in its public functioning. Culture, in this sense, is all about the way meaning, as it is being conceived, is mediated through our highly technological society, its dense cities, its all-enveloping capitalistic structures, its bureaucracies, and its omnipresent media. It is about how all of these facets of modernization shape how meaning comes to be understood. Politics is our window into culture through which we see, as Craig Gay put it, a peoples' "most basic assumptions about the nature of the world and their most cherished aspirations for life within it." It is this consensus about the meaning of the modern world that comes to be viewed as being normal and, therefore, that develops the status of being normative. It is this, then, that even takes on the weight of being ethical, which, of course, it often is not.

The engagement of evangelical faith with culture understood in this kind of way is a complex, many-sided story and one that would take us far beyond our present topic. However, as diffuse and far-ranging as this theme is, it is also integral to our topic. I therefore need to sketch this out briefly in the most bare-bones, rudimentary way in order to make a single point. That point is that for many reasons, and over a long period of time, our nation, bit by bit, has left behind the moral world it once inhabited and has now taken up residence in a therapeutic world as its substitute. And what is true of the nation as a whole is true, apparently, of the evangelical sector as well. In both cases—both in the nation and in the evangelical soul—the domain of "obedience to the unenforceable" is collapsing. If this is true, it explains what evangelical faith needs to do if it is to engage culture effectively and that, in turn, has implications for the evangelical engagement of the political process.

From Moral to Therapeutic

When we look at American life today, I have argued elsewhere,[13] the indications are that, in our minds at least, we are leaving behind the older moral world. This is evident in many ways but not least in four, closely related and fundamental shifts. We have shifted from thinking about virtues to thinking about values, from thinking about nature to thinking about self, from thinking about character to thinking about personality, and from thinking about guilt to thinking about shame. Of these, only two can engage us here, the shifts regarding virtues and nature.

Virtues, as I am thinking of them here, are aspects of the Good, of what is enduringly right and true for all people in all generations and times. They are the moral norms that are applicable both to private and public life.

It is true that there has been debate about what these norms are. It is also true that in a postmodern context absolute norms are rejected by most people, in America apparently by 65 percent.[14] It is also the case that Scripture itself rarely speaks of virtues in quite this sense, but it does speak of moral excellence as this is rooted in, and reflects, the character of God. This is, after all, still a moral universe, a universe sustained in its moral structure by God himself, and all people are held accountable for knowing the difference between right and wrong (e.g. Matt 12:36; Rom 1:18–20; 2:16; 1 Cor 4:5).

In our context, though, this fabric has melted into highly privatized values. Values are simply what are important to the individual, and we now treat values in a value-free way. Values represent the moral talk of those who inhabit a relativistic universe.

This shift from thinking about virtues to thinking about values goes hand-in-hand with the other shift, from thinking about nature to thinking about the self.

For centuries in the West, we have thought that what distinguishes humans from mere animals has been the possession of human nature, whether simply in a general form or, more specifically, in its Christian form as the *imago Dei*. But first in philosophy, then in biology, and now across

---

13. David F. Wells, *Losing Our Virtue: Why the Church Must Recover Its Moral Vision* (Grand Rapids: Eerdmans, 1998).

14. The Barna Group, "Most Adults Feel Accepted by God," n.p.

the whole intellectual front, the idea of human nature is under siege. It is being repudiated because, it is said, there is no evidence for saying that such a thing exists, or because it is part of an obsolete understanding that divided reality into that which is natural and that which is supernatural, or simply because it is insulting, suggesting that individuals are merely exponents of this common substratum called nature, rather than being unique selves. We have therefore shifted from thinking about nature to thinking about the self. And the self is that juncture within each person where personal narrative, private insights, and individual intuitions all come together in a combination that is unique to each person.

In 2003, a comprehensive, sophisticated, European-based study called *World Values Survey*[15] was published, which surveyed the operating assumption of 80 percent of the world's people. The bottom line for Western, modernized countries is that the overwhelming majority in all such countries have become deeply self-focused, and in the United States this development is among the most aggravated. This reorganization of life around the self is not juxtaposed against, or consciously opposed to, the older ideas about human nature. The reality, though, is that one waxes while the other wanes and, in fact, these older ideas about human nature are simply vanishing. And as the self is made central, not only is human nature rejected but so, too, are tradition and all forms of authority, be they moral or religious, which have gone hand-in-hand with the traditional way of thinking of human beings. "The contemporary climate is therapeutic," wrote Christopher Lasch as this transformation unfolded, "not religious. People today hunger not for personal salvation, let alone the restoration of an earlier golden age, but for the feeling, the momentary illusion, of personal well-being, health, and psychic security."[16]

Talk about virtues belongs in a moral world where we also speak about a human nature, which has moral capacities. Talk about values belongs in a therapeutic world where we speak about the self, a self in which the old moral capacities have either vanished or become irrelevant. Yet, while moral norms have disappeared, personal rights, ironically, are multiplying. That is the anomaly.

---

15. World Values Survey: The Most Comprehensive Investigation of Political and Sociological Change, online: http://www.worldvaluessurvey.org/.

16. Christopher Lasch, *The Culture of Narcissism: American Life in an Age of Diminishing Expectations* (New York: Norton, 1978), 7.

In a moral world, life is about self-restraint and self-sacrifice for moral reasons; in a therapeutic world, life is about self-esteem and self-realization for therapeutic reasons, and it is about pursuing self-interest and self-expression. It is about the way we present the self in public with a mind to how we are perceived. It is therefore about gain of one kind or another.

In our Western societies, we *want* to think only in terms of the self, not of nature. We *want* to structure our lives in terms of values but not of virtues. The reason is that while we are inhabiting this psychological world, we are freed from all of the moral obligations that belong in the older religious world, and so our freedom remains unqualified because it is unrestrained. And yet, our sense of entitlements, our sense of rights, is quite as acute as once was the sense of obligation to moral norms.

While it is true, Samuel Huntington has said, that the West in general has achieved undisputed world dominance politically, militarily, and economically, it is also true that the West is "a civilization in decline, its share of world political, economic, and military power going down relative to that of other civilizations."[17] And there is now a prolific literature that has sought to illumine this kind of decline in the West, not least the ways in which this decline is evident in America. In a typical statement, though one that is a little less measured than Huntington's, Jim Black has said that it "is no longer an original claim to say that the nations of Europe and America are in an advanced state of decline today."[18] He goes on to say that government "has turned predator, pouring the wealth of the nation down the rat hole of debt; and our social resources are being depleted at an astonishing pace."[19]

It would be comforting to be able to conclude that, despite this drift into an amoral therapeutic realm where self-interest trumps moral considerations, the born-again world has become a major counter-weight. Unfortunately, its own loss of theological bearings, not to mention its own enculturation, has produced ways of being Christian that are not significantly different from our ways of being typically cultural. And that is what seems to explain the fact that when Barna compared how the born-again

---

17. Samuel P. Huntington, *The Clash of Civilizations: Remaking of the World Order* (New York: Touchstone, 1997), 81–82.

18. Jim Nelson Black, *When Nations Die: Ten Warning Signs of a Culture in Crisis* (Wheaton: Tyndale, 1994), 10.

19. Ibid., 11.

world lives on an ethical plane, and how self-described secularists live, he could find few differences. In fact, the only major difference is that born-againers are slightly less likely to be involved in music piracy but beyond that the differences disappear.[20] If these figures are accurate, then we have a further reason to think, as Os Guinness has said, that while Christian faith is privately engaging, it has become publicly irrelevant and, not least, ethically so.

Moral Restraint and Christian Faith

Where, then, is the moral restraint going to come from as the twin impulses of freedom and equality work their way through our culture and then are given political form? When these impulses walk hand-in-hand with what is morally right, they contribute to what has been unique and extraordinary about America and when they do not, when these impulses are unhooked from what is morally right, they have the power to undo what has been so good about America. Where, then, is the evangelical church in all of this?

The role of Christian faith in society is to ask for what is right by way of public policies and programs, to do what is good, and to act as a restraint, wherever possible, on what is wrong. Much is encompassed in this multi-faceted role. Not least is this true in terms of the last component, that of restraining what is wrong. So, if this is an obligation, what is it that evangelicals and born-againers think needs to be restrained?

The most important things that were on the evangelical mind in January, 2008, according to Barna, were the following: 94 percent cited abortion as the principal political issue in the presidential election, followed by personal indebtedness (81 percent), the content of movies and television (79 percent), and then the advocacy and practice of homosexuality (75 percent). They were quite unconcerned about HIV/AIDS. In the more general category of the born-again, 79 percent cited as their principal political issue personal indebtedness, 78 percent said poverty was a pressing concern, and 77 percent listed HIV/AIDS.[21] In short, the ethical

20. The Barna Group, "Fewer Than 1 in 10 Teenagers Believe That Music Piracy Is Morally Wrong," *Barna Update*, April 26, 2004, n.p., online: http://www.barna.org/barna-update/article/5-barna-update/139-fewer-than-1-in-10-teenagers-believe-that-music-piracy-is-morally-wrong.

21. The Barna Group, "Americans Describe Their Moral and Social Concerns, Including Abortion and Homosexuality," *Barna Update*, January 21, 2008, n.p., online:

issues that this combined and large sector of the electorate cited as being on the front burner of the political election, as far as they were concerned, were private debt and poverty followed by "family values" issues—HIV/AIDS, abortion, premarital sex and its depiction in the movies, homosexuality and its promotion. This, interestingly enough, is also close to the overall national consensus.

So what might we expect along these or any other fronts from evangelical and born-again political involvement? In thinking about this, we have to balance the biblical understanding of the greatness of human life as created and, as Blaise Pascall said, its matching wretchedness. It is not the one without the other, it is both at the same time. This wretchedness is its pervasive fallenness, and this fallenness works hand-in-hand with the culture, which makes this fallenness both public and normative. This, in fact, is what the Bible has in mind by worldliness. Worldliness is all of the ways in which our culture makes sin look normal and makes the righteousness of God's character seem strange because it is so alien to this life.

However, culture also reflects this duality of human life, both in its greatness and its wretchedness. There is an appeal that can be made to human nature which is still made in the *imago Dei*, still lives in the world in which God's unyielding righteousness is "revealed from heaven against all ungodliness and unrighteousness of men" (Rom 1:18), and is still troubled by its own conscience (Rom 2:14–15). There may, then, be some victories because there is an appeal that can be made to this side of human life. However, the central ideas in the prevailing culture are rarely susceptible to any political fixes for any length of time. If the culture does not change, campaigns launched on behalf of pressing ethical concerns are not likely to have much success. It is simply too hard for most people to swim up stream for too long.

This culture is about the set of life-assumptions that lie beneath these ethical affronts, and it is these which need most to be changed. This culture is tempered less by law, legislation, and politics than by a moral sensibility. This sensibility is most effectively promoted by Christian example, by osmosis, and by persuasion in the workplace. If it is only being shouted out in the churches, or on Christian television, it will not be heard in the culture where the changes really need to happen.

---

http://www.barna.org/barna-update/article/13-culture/50-americans-describe-their-moral-and-social-concerns-including-abortion-and-homosexuality.

In this engagement, then, Christians who are biblically-minded bring both an orientation to what life should be like as well as a subdued understanding about the prospects for transforming the nation given what fallen human nature is actually like. They bring a vision of what human nature was made to be but also a subdued understanding about human nature as it now lies corrupted. It is this fact that is a constant reminder that the kingdom of God is different from the kingdoms of this world and that attempts at "trying to dress up the Christian way of the cross to look like self-interested American foreign policy," as Allen Hilton puts it, "are bound to end in frustration."[22] Aside from the cross, modest amelioration of life's ethical raggedness seems a more realistic outcome to seek than to hope for root-and-branch, radical transformation. Small gains should be counted as victories, rather than defeat being pronounced over anything less than total conquest. This may seem like a moment of small-thinking but, in fact, had we had such caution about human prospects, our nation would not have embarked on some of its most costly, and most reckless public experiments, and we would not be about to do something similar under the Obama administration. Had this kind of Christian caution been expressed and heeded, the nation would have saved itself an immense outlay in expenditures which could have been put to more productive purposes.

This confidence in changing the whole American landscape has actually been long in the making, and it is rooted in the Enlightenment assumptions about the limitless capacities of human nature to improve life as well as of government's ability to be an instrument in this cause. Modern media, especially television, has had a hand in shaping this too, because of its excessive preoccupation with stories about life that call for solutions. This has now become a part of the secularization of our life and of how our expectations about government are shaped. We have come to think that every problem has a solution and that national problems are simply a combination of all of our regional and individual problems.

As a result, we are developing an almost boundless belief in the capacity of government to eliminate problems by managing them, and while some problems can be eliminated by wise, judicious programs, many simply cannot because they are rooted in a corrupted human na-

---

22. Allen R. Hilton, "Who Are We? Being Christian in an Age of Americanism," in *Anxious about Empire: Theological Essays on the New Global Realities* (Grand Rapids: Brazos, 2004), 155.

ture whose capacities for change are not boundless. "The experience of history," writes Don Eberly, "suggests that heavily hyped social reforms aimed at rebuilding a moral society through the ballot box, whether liberal or conservative, deserve skepticism."[23]

Nevertheless, government has continued to expand, programs continue to be added, the cost continues to mount, and as the Obama administration begins, much, much more is planned. The national debt has soared and it is going to soar far higher.

The astounding growth of the state, especially in the post-World War II period, has had many natural causes. Indeed, it is the case that after every national crisis—whether it is economic in nature, such as the Depression of the 1930s; or social, such as the Civil Rights movement of the 1960s; or related to matters of security, such as the emergence of global terrorism in the 1990s—the government's agencies, reach, and size have grown. And, in addition to these types of emergency, there is the fact that in the globalized context in which we live, with its complexities of trade, tariffs, and immigration, more is asked of the government by way of seeing that rules and laws are observed than used to be the case, and so the state has inevitably grown larger. Yet while some of this growth may have quite natural explanations, it is also the case that there is now little resistance to the state expanding far beyond the roles that it has filled in the past. And the reason is that while individual politicians disappoint us, and while political campaigns often aggravate us quite as much as they enlighten us, we nevertheless continue to have almost boundless expectations as to what government can and should be doing for us.

In fact, the state has never had a larger footprint than it does today. It has never loomed so large over individuals, businesses, towns, cites, and farms. Its tentacles reach deeply into every corner of American life. What we have today, I strongly suspect, would scarcely have been imaginable to those who wrote our Constitution.

And if we are content to sustain this massive superstructure, as we are, it is because of the hopes we continue to nurture about what government can do for American citizens. That it all runs in the red, that a mountain of debt is piling up, and that America is now technically bankrupt is water that runs off the American back. This, in fact, is also how many Americans live at a personal level. In the first ten months of 2007, for example, and

---

23. Don E. Eberly, *Restoring the Good Society: A New Vision for Politics and Culture* (Grand Rapids: Baker, 1994), 74.

before the spending spree of Christmas, Americans wracked up $50 billion in credit card debt.[24]

It is no wonder, then, that personal debt, much of it in mortgages that could not be paid back, was a significant issue in the 2008 presidential campaign and produced a national economic crisis by year's end. But, who, one wonders, is responsible for all of this personal debt? Congress? The banks who made the loans available? The interest rates? This issue of personal indebtedness was only turned into a political issue because the national spending spree, driven by those with an enormous sense of entitlement and a correspondingly diminished sense of self-restraint, happened to coincide with the same lack of restraint by lending institutions, and the result then endangered the entire economy. It is a political issue only to the degree that the failure of Congress to exercise adequate oversight allowed it to damage the economy. We have to ask, how it is that imprudent borrowers, and incautious banks, can somehow shift their responsibility for what has happened onto the political process? It is borrowers, be they individual or institutional, who are responsible for their own debts even if lenders have made it so easy to acquire those debts.

It is this kind of atmosphere in which responsibility becomes diminished that explains a number of government actions. A prime example is the attempt to abolish poverty launched by Lyndon Johnson's "Great Society" programs in the 1965. In the three decades which followed, they cost the country $3.5 trillion and yet the poverty level was at a higher level at the end of this period than when the program was first launched. The poverty level is still at a higher level today. And much the same happened in the gaudy welfare programs that had accompanied the anti-poverty program. While there were some who were helped by these programs, they also produced as a byproduct an underclass of people who were unwilling or unable to compete in the marketplace and so had become more or less permanently dependent on the handout. Children born to those on welfare—and soon an overwhelming majority of such children were found to be born out of wedlock—found that they had been born into permanent poverty. It was not that the objectives of this ideology were wrong. After all, who wants poverty? Who does not think that it would be better if no one were poor? Who wants life's tragedies? Who does not want people to be provided with all the help they need in overcoming

---

24. "How to Recover From Holiday 'Debt Hangover,'" *MSNBC*, January 3, 2008, online: http://www.msnbc.msn.com/id/22476874.

their misfortunes? The question, though, is what we can realistically expect government to do.

In fact, both the Great Society anti-poverty programs, as well as many of the welfare programs prior to their reform, were significant failures. The reason is that they rested upon an understanding of human nature so naïve as to be breathtaking, coupled with a substitution of an enduring moral world by a therapeutic regime. And added to this is the fact that mediating structures in society, such as the family and the church, have been bypassed by an omni-competent state intent on doing good, a state which does not understand that there are maladies of the human spirit which no government program can fix. Exercises in compassion which misunderstandings like this inspire actually end up undermining civic virtue as Christopher Lasch has argued. This compassion both "degrades" the victims as they are reduced to being "objects of pity," he says, and it degrades the "would-be benefactors" because they "find it easier to pity their fellow citizens than to hold them up to impersonal standards, attainment of which would entitle them to respect." We do, indeed, pity those who suffer but "we reserve respect for those who refuse to exploit their suffering for the purposes of pity," Lasch says.[25]

But where, one wonders, has the evangelical church been in all of this? And where is it now that the Obama administration is about to launch the country into depths of debt the likes of which we have never seen before? Why have we not heard evangelical leaders making the case for self-restraint, for prudence, and against our mounting national debt? Why have they not voiced their skepticism about the Enlightenment naïvetés that underlie these mammoth programs? Why has a more subdued understanding about human prospects, coupled with a more soaring view of human worth, not been articulated more widely and persuasively?

Peter Wehner, former deputy assistant to President George W. Bush, has said that, "the rhetoric of candidates needs to be principled but civil, inviting rather than aggressive, and radiate grace instead of invoking apocalyptic warnings."[26] This is good advice to candidates and it is good advice to the church, too. However, before this advice can be followed, the

---

25. Christopher Lasch, *The Revolt of the Elites and the Betrayal of Democracy* (New York: Norton, 1995), 105.

26. Peter Wehner, "Among Evangelicals, a Transformation," *National Review*, December 31, 2007, 32, online: http://nrd.nationalreview.com/article/?q=ZTRmZTE2OTc3YjlmMGQ4YzBlYTYxODYzMmQ4OTdiMDY=.

church or, at least, the evangelical corner of it, must first recover its voice for, until it has a voice, it can hardly begin to think about how to use it.

And there will be no such voice without a deeper understanding of how important moral character is in the nation's collective life, a character that is not simply private but also public, and not an outcome at all of the political process but its necessary foundation. It is all about the "obedience to the unenforceable."

However, for those who know Christ, so much more is expected than just this natural virtue. What is expected is what today, if Barna's numbers are correct, is conspicuous by its absence. What we are not seeing is a deep, fibrous, winsome Christ-like character, the kind of character that does not buckle in the public square and does not make alliances that are unseemly and damaging. Freed from the intellectual conventions, the party interests, the tribal rivalries for power, this kind of character is what actually enables Christians to begin to think big thoughts about how different society could be, to be bold and courageous in its reform. Evangelical political engagement is actually less about politics and more about moral engagement. However, this engagement is quite impossible if the needed character is not there. Until this kind of moral excellence, this deep integrity, is the first thing that comes to mind whenever the word *evangelical* is heard, evangelical political involvement is not going to amount to more than it does now.

2

The Travails of Evangelical Politics

Paul Marshall

INTRODUCTION

IN THIS ESSAY I will try to explore some theological reasons for the problems in contemporary evangelical politics. Of course, there are many more than theological reasons for these problems. Also, it is very doubtful that tens of millions of diverse, active, pragmatic, and questioning people can be of one political mind. But theology is important. Before proceeding further, I need to make some comments on the nature of politics and of evangelicalism.

POLITICS AS CALLING

It is important to emphasize some of the requirements of politics as a Christian calling. The meaning of politics is, of course, much disputed. Often "politics" is used to refer to manipulation, lust for power, double dealing, and outright graft. This is well captured in Ambrose Bierce's *The Devil's Dictionary*: "POLITICS, n. A strife of interests masquerading as a contest of principles. The conduct of public affairs for private advantage."[1] On the other hand, John Calvin remarked, doubtless with some exaggeration, that "civil authority is a calling not only holy and lawful before God, but also the most sacred and by far the most honorable of all callings in the whole life of mortal men."[2] It is a calling with

---

1. Ambrose Bierce, *The Devil's Dictionary* (Minneapolis: Filiquarian, 2006), 191.
2. John Calvin, *Institutes of the Christian Religion*, edited by J. T. McNeill, translated by F. Battles (Philadelphia: Westminster, 1960), 1490.

distinctive demands. Perhaps this may be illustrated by a TV program. At a time of discussion as to whether there should be a paperback version of Salman Rushdie's *The Satanic Verses*, whose author had been declared an apostate worthy of death (and several of whose translators had been murdered), many civil libertarians defended an absolute right to publish freely. In the first segment of the program they demanded that the government remove all barriers to the book's free publication and wide circulation. They said this was their political position.

The second segment had relatives of hostages held in Lebanon. They felt that the government should not stand on abstract principle, but negotiate the captives' release. They called this their political position.

The producer had a rare brainwave, or an insight into politics. The third segment brought both civil libertarians and hostage supporters together. The interviewer then asked the hard question; that is, the real *political* question: "If the terms of hostage release was suppression of *The Satanic Verses*, would you do it?" (Such a demand had been made.) "What if the hostages would be killed if the book were not withdrawn?"

This question produced momentary silence. The civil libertarians waffled. None were willing to acquiesce in the death of a known person to further their cause, especially if that person's wife were sitting opposite, on television. The relatives were more direct. "Absolutely yes! Free real flesh and blood human beings, not printed pages."

The discussion continued, but now in wayward fashion. The diamond-hard moment had come and gone. Briefly, the question was no longer an abstract demand but a real question, a genuine *political* question. No longer a debate about one single ideal, one demand, one good, nor even two ideals, demands, goods, or assertions. It now addressed many ideals, many goods, many demands, many assertions, *together*. These different demands were inherently not achievable at the same time.

This illuminates a central fact of politics: the difference between governing and interest group pressure, between governing and ideals, between governing and demands. An interest group can push for one thing without having to face others' demands, and is not held accountable by those whose policies it may hurt. Idealists do not have to deal with the people that oppose them; they only have to claim that their ideal is right.

But governing a country, state, or school board necessarily requires dealing with many demands and ideals at the same time. This is true not only of short-sighted, selfish demands but even of legitimate, proper demands. This, *inter alia*, is a feature of politics.

THE MEANING OF "EVANGELICAL"

Of course, the word "evangelical" is also notoriously difficult to define. But, if we adopt David Bebbington's widely used description, it is "conversionist"—believing that people's lives need to be personally changed; "activist"—affirming that the gospel must be expressed in life; "biblicist"—having a high view of the Bible and its authority for the church; and "crucicentrist"—stressing Christ's sacrifice on the cross.[3]

It is important to note that these stresses are not themselves a full theological system and that they can be compatible with a range of other doctrines. Hence, we can speak easily of evangelical Anglicans or Lutherans, and perhaps even of evangelical Orthodox or Catholics. *Time* magazine self-consciously listed two Catholics in its list of twenty-five leading evangelicals.[4] The *Economist* plausibly took Senator Sam Brownback, a convert to Catholicism, to symbolize growing evangelical international activism on religious freedom, sex trafficking, AIDS, Sudan, and North Korea.[5]

EVANGELICALISM IS A PARTIAL DOCTRINE: A THEOLOGICAL TENDENCY

Given the nature of politics and of evangelicalism, many problems arise when activists leap into the political fray armed only with the resources of evangelicalism itself, giving them a weight they cannot bear.

They do not take us far in understanding politics, a practice that requires at least some grasp of the nature of history, government, law, justice, freedom, rights, mercy, violence and war, not to mention the difficulties of prudential decision making between a bad choice and a worse one. In the U.S. we must also struggle with the nature and demands of

---

3. David W. Bebbington, *Evangelicalism in Modern Britain: A History from the 1730s to the 1980s* (London: Unwin Hyman, 1989).

4. "The 25 Most Influential Evangelicals in America," *Time*, February 7, 2005, online: http://www.time.com/time/covers/1101050207/photoessay/.

5. "Sam Brownback on the March." *The Economist*, March 9, 2006.

democracy—not least, of the proper accountability of political leaders to a population whose views may not be their own.[6]

Historically, evangelicalism has produced laudable results, not least in providing a commitment to religious freedom predating the Enlightenment, and in developing an ethic of personal responsibility that produced the engaged civil society that Tocqueville so admired. But it also produces major problems.

ANABAPTISM

One is the disproportionate influence of Anabaptist thought on evangelicalism. Since Anabaptist thought is itself a Free Church tradition, it can lend itself readily to evangelical appropriation. But, in itself, though with a stress on non-violence, it has little to say on many political problems.

This shows in discussions of what is called "peacemaking." In international affairs, advocates urge cultural sensitivity, direct contact with others, learning about others, and genuine listening to the other. All these are worthy goals. But they are not new, and, along "peacemaking" in foreign policy, have been advocated for several millennia.

The U.S., like almost every other country in the world, has made it its business to recruit highly talented people, train them and immerse them in the languages and cultures of others, and seek to ensure that they are equipped in the arts of negotiation, compromise, and, in short, peacemaking. We call such people diplomats, their office, the Department of State, and their boss, the Secretary of State, is the highest-ranking non-elected figure in the U.S. government. The Department of State is charged as the major body in how we relate to other countries. We may have major problems in how the State Department conducts itself, but to act as if our government has never given a priority to peacemaking is essentially to admit that one has never given much attention to how our government actually operates.

Anabaptism, of course, has many virtues, including a stress on the church's own communal role in addressing social problems, a commitment to the poor, and, historically at least, a deep suspicion of government. Traditionally, it has also usually opposed the strong secularizing

---

6. I have sought to describe elements of Christian political thought in my *God and the Constitution: Christianity and American Politics* (Lanham, MD: Rowman & Littlefield, 2002).

tendencies that are, in America, now usually found on the left. But it is not a full political doctrine.

ANABAPTISM AND THE LEFT

One consequence is that we now often see, with figures such as Tony Campolo and Jim Wallis, a fusion of Anabaptist views with leftist politics, an appropriation fraught with contradictions. These two quite different streams of thought and commitment do not sit together easily.

As noted, the Anabaptist view has often portrayed the state as "Caesar," as a realm separate from Christ, and, in our post-lapsarian condition, inextricably intertwined with the threat of force. Hence, it was to be avoided where possible and/or addressed prophetically. But leftist politics, while suspicious of military and police power, frequently calls for expansive government involvement in income redistribution, welfare reform, medical support, and a host of other social ills.

If these two are combined, then "Caesar," the realm of coercion, is urged to take over ever larger swathes of society. I once heard a representative of this view invoke the common trope of juxtaposing the discussion of politics in Romans 13 with the description of the Beast in Revelation 13, and so denouncing "Caesar" as sort of the antichrist. Later, he called on the U.S. government to institute a national health plan, apparently oblivious of the fact that he was calling on the antichrist to monopolize health care—a position that is, to say the very least, theologically and otherwise problematic.

Also, much modern American legal doctrine has interpreted the First Amendment to mean that everything government touches must be, or must be made, religion free, with the result that, to the degree that the government is increasingly involved in society, as all modern governments are, society itself must become religion free. Hence, currently, a commitment to an expansive state tends to be a commitment to a secular society.

OTHER PROBLEMS OF EVANGELICAL POLITICS

The paucity of evangelical political reflection currently hampers responsible political engagement through its casual use of the Bible, its activism, and its stress on prophecy and prophets. This results in:

The Travails of Evangelical Politics

- A lack of political thought
- Biblicism
- Activism
- An overestimation of "prophecy"
- A lack of real politics

Lack of Christian Political Thought

Take the example of Jim Wallis's *God's Politics*.[7] It, in very American pragmatist fashion, leaps to what are often called "issues." That is, it describes purported problems in society that the state is then, without argument, presumed to be required to solve, or about which it should at least act. The state is portrayed simply as a means to achieve our desired goals.[8]

Contrary to reflection in the Protestant, Catholic, Eastern Orthodox, and Oriental Orthodox traditions, he does not discuss the proper nature and role of God's servant, government, under God's sovereignty. Most Christian reflection has worried about the fact that, in a state of sin, government is often a coercive agent—it forces people to do things by threat of violence (think about what would happen if there were no penalty for not paying taxes)—and that this properly and necessarily limits the range of things we should want or expect it to do.[9] Wallis does give us some theological reflection on non-violence, but on the rest of his claims, almost nothing.

Like all too many on the "Christian right," he sees government simply as an agent to solve whatever problems or create whatever social good he might like it to. The result is a naïve pragmatism wherein the government is seen simply as a tool to solve our problems.

Hence, for example, Wallis spends a very great deal of time expounding God's concern for the poor, and says that the Bible says more on this than it does on many issues of current concern to the "Christian Right."

---

7. Jim Wallis, *God's Politics: Why the Right Gets It Wrong and the Left Doesn't Get It* (San Francisco: HarperCollins, 2005).

8. An earlier version of the following discussion is given in my "Jim Wallis' Politics—or Lack Thereof," *Review of Faith and International Affairs,* March 15, 2006.

9. For a good overview of earlier Christian reflection on these matters, see Oliver O'Donovan and Joan Lockwood O'Donovan, edsitors, *From Irenaeus to Grotius: A Sourcebook in Christian Political Thought 100–1625* (Grand Rapids: Eerdmans, 2000).

He is entirely correct. But what might this mean politically? If our focus is on politics then our question is not what God cares about *per se* but what God calls governments to do. On this he is silent.

Biblicism

Similarly, evangelicals frequently move quickly from the biblical text, whether on economics or the nature of the family, to contemporary political prescription while hardly addressing the entirety of the biblical story.

One common example is the move from the forgiveness of debts required in Israel's Sabbath and Jubilee years to current programs for the forgiveness of Third World debt. Let me be clear that I have much sympathy for such debt reduction, but Israel's Jubilee was more than a redistributive mechanism.

It was ordained as the response of a covenanted community reordering its internal affairs in an explicit liturgical process beginning on the Day of Atonement, when Israel commemorated God's forgiveness of its own debts.

The Jubilee certainly has implications for current policies on debt and illegal immigration—it implies that no debts, or crimes, are absolute obligations to be repaid come what may (a feature helping shape our modern bankruptcy laws). But it is no blueprint for modern policies to forgive Third World debt if, for example, such forgiveness ends up alleviating the fiscal problems of, and so strengthening, thugs such as Robert Mugabe in Zimbabwe.

Also, if this aspect of Israel's life is normative for modern economics, then why not also other areas? The Jubilee was to be followed immediately by two years of abstaining from planting crops, in order to emphasize Israel's total dependence on God, but I have not seen Christians advocate this in international relations.

Israel also allowed little religious freedom: followers of Moloch were to be stoned to death (something to be remembered in dialog with Muslims about the punitive parts of their scriptures). Should we imitate Joshua's call for war in the name of God or Leviticus's admonition to kill adulterers?

If not, then we need to justify following a truncated version of the Jubilee but not other practices, and, more broadly, suggest how we should move hermeneutically from the Israelites' as a covenanted, land-based, tribal people to a multi-religious, service-based, federal, and otherwise diverse polity such as modern America.

As Calvin noted in the *Institutes*, "The law of God given through Moses is (not) dishonored when it is abrogated and new laws are preferred to it . . . for the Lord . . . did not give that law to be proclaimed among all nations and to be in force everywhere. Rather we must make our laws with regard to the condition of times, place and nation."[10]

Activism and Bipolarity

Another consequence of this approach to the Bible, combined with evangelical activism, is imaging politics as a crusade, often producing a mountain of engagement built on a minimum of theology. Several years ago, former Christian right activists Cal Thomas and Ed Dobson criticized their own previous hubris when founding the Moral Majority: "We were on our way to changing America" . . . "We had the power to right every wrong and cure every ill."[11]

Of course, this early triumphalism naturally met its counterpart in later defeatism and so they lamented, "The moral landscape of America has become worse . . . Two decades after conservative Christians charged into the political arena, bringing new voters and millions of dollars with them in hopes of transforming the culture through political power, it must be acknowledged that we have failed."[12]

This manic-depressive, bipolar syndrome was nothing new in evangelical activism. The Christian Coalition and the Moral Majority fit a historical pattern of political passivity that is eventually provoked by fear of secular intrusion into crusade. The troops are rallied in a movement whose dominant metaphors are military, salvific, or eschatological, calling for battles to "save" society. The crusade usually has several years of activity until the apparent resistance of the world to reform leads to disappointment, sometimes degenerating into cynicism. It is not a very biblical hope.

---

10. Calvin, *Institutes*, 1505.

11. Cal Thomas and Ed Dobson, *Blinded by Might: Can the Religious Right Save America?* (Grand Rapids: Zondervan, 1999), 22.

12. Ibid, 23.

God and Governing

Overestimation of Prophecy

Activism combines easily with a predilection for "prophecy" that is common, though in different forms, on the left and right. Pat Robertson's pronouncements that Ariel Sharon's stroke was God's punishment for his concessions to the Palestinians, and that the U.S. should assassinate Venezuelan President Hugo Chavez, obviously claim a remarkably detailed knowledge of God's intentions in the complexities of human history.

The same is true of eschatological speculation attempting to match biblical texts with current events. This climaxes in ruminations on conflict in the Middle East, especially attacks on Israel or wars around Iraq, which fortuitously contains ancient Babylon. Prophetic proponents outline the eschatological scenario of the month and, in the past, passively awaited the unfolding of the divine calendar; or else, particularly since the Israeli-Arab war of 1967, support the policies of, usually, the U.S. or Israel, believing that these policies might fulfill the prophecy.

However, even apart from its problematic mode of interpretation, *this approach gives no guide to action*. For example, the fact that Isaiah says God delivered Israel into the Babylonians' hands would give no reason to support the Mesopotamians' enslavement of Israel or their destruction of the temple. In the nature of the case, prophecies, in the limited sense of predictions about the future, can provide no guidance, political or otherwise, on what we are called to do. We are called to follow commandments, not prophecies.

The Partiality of Prophets

One pervasive and pernicious pattern is to portray the prophet as the key political actor (and often then implicitly to appropriate the prophetic mantle for the proponent). For example, Wallis writes, "The place to begin to understand the politics of God is with the prophets."[13] There is no wisp of an argument justifying this unusual contention. A novel doctrine is asserted as indubitable fact. But the Bible itself, of course, does not begin with the prophets, but with Genesis, as does most historical Christian reflection. In fact, the prophets drew, *inter alia*, on the Torah, acknowledging that they challenged rulers not on their own feelings of injustice on the basis of God's previously given law.

---

13. Wallis, *God's Politics*, 32.

The Travails of Evangelical Politics

The prophets are important to politics, often as critics of lawgivers, judges, elders, and kings, such as Moses or David, who held divinely appointed political office. But their vital role cannot substitute for understanding the actual burdens of legal and political responsibility itself. If we take prophets as our political role model, then we overstress this critical outsider's role. Max Weber suggested the prophets might well be understood as forerunners of a free press, in which case the contemporary inheritors of their mantle would be journalists and pundits rather than pastors or prelates.[14]

I have myself committed to journalism, and think it a wonderful thing, but it is no substitute for government.

Often such modern "prophets," like those from Hollywood, pass over the real problems faced by government and politicians. They present them instead with pictures of ideals and societies to achieve rather than real guidance for governing the varied and brawling people they actually govern day to day. It is as if, when parents asked for advice on rearing their children, they were presented simply with a description of what an ideal child is. Their reply would be, "I know what kids are supposed to be, but that tells me nothing. I need advice on what, today, I should do with the little monsters I actually have."

Prudence and Statesmanship

A "prophetic" politics also underplays the importance of prudence and questions of political virtue and character. Classical (and Christian) political thought discusses prudence, and its political expression, statesmanship.

Unfortunately, mentioning prudence in the modern world invites misunderstanding, since much of its meaning in Christian thought has been lost. It is often treated simply as utilitarianism or pragmatism; as judging an act merely by its consequences. It is sometimes merged with "realism," especially in international relations, and treated as flinty-eyed self-interest, or timidity and self-preservation—the preserve of the small-minded. In colloquial use it is well captured in comedian Dana Carvey's

---

14. Max Weber, "Religious Groups (The Sociology of Religion)," in *Economy and Society: An Outline of Interpretive Sociology*, vol. 1, part 2, edited by Guenther Roth and Claus Wittich (Berkeley: University of California Press, 1978), 399–634.

parodies of George H. W. Bush contemplating action but then withdrawing with a mumbled, "But wouldn't be prudent, wouldn't be prudent."

In some Christian circles it is considered the opposite of genuine Christian ethics, the evasion of absolute commands, and a refusal to trust that the consequences of our actions lie ultimately in God's hands. To quote Josef Pieper, "To the contemporary mind, prudence seems less a prerequisite to goodness than an evasion of it."[15]

But there are good reasons why prudence has been considered a virtue. One of its dimensions is a true grasp of the world—what it is and what is possible within it. This knowledge concerns not only the universal conditions of human life but also a grasp of particular situations, of the contingencies of our historical moment. This, in turn, requires not merely the ability to recall a mountain of facts, but a willingness to be taught by experience, to listen to and take advice, openness to the unexpected and good judgment about the future. These are not solely matters of skill and discipline, though they are involved, but also concern for the condition of our heart and soul. Uncertainty underlies action in the political world and no amount of knowledge or piety will change this, so courage is also part of prudence.

If we are to learn prudence and other political virtues, it is important to look to intrinsically political examples.

Lack of Politics

However, a stress on prophecy also disproportionately highlights the roles of Christians *outside* the political arena. Hence, in discussing the end of Apartheid in South Africa, Jim Wallis focuses on Archbishop Desmond Tutu's worthy role.

But why pick a bishop as a role model rather than those other two South African, Christian, Nobel Peace Prize winners, Nelson Mandela and F. W. de Klerk, who not only rejected Apartheid but took up the staggeringly difficult political task of leading a bitterly divided country through the painful and ethically fraught compromises required for an actual peaceful transfer of power? Mandela then took up the equally difficult task of leading the country through the minefields of its fractious

---

15. Josef Pieper, *The Four Cardinal Virtues: Prudence, Justice, Fortitude, Temperance*, translated by Richard and Clara Winston et al. (South Bend: University of Notre Dame Press 1966), 4.

early years. If you are a Christian looking for political role models, why not look to politicians rather than to a bishop?

We should look, not to self-declared prophets, but to actual political practitioners.

In this anniversary season, William Wilberforce and his fellows serve as one great example, of course, but there are more recent ones.

Leaving aside the Calvinist founders of the Red Cross and the shapers of the Geneva and Hague Conventions on the laws of war, two of the world-scale major political programs of the last century are the United Nations and the European Union. Often the formation of the Universal Declaration of Human Rights is portrayed as a standoff between Western liberals and Eastern communists. But the late John Humphrey, who produced the first draft of the Universal Declaration of Human Rights, noted, "it seemed at times that the chief protagonists in the conference room were the Roman Catholics and the Communists, with the latter a poor second."[16] Those Catholics, including Jacques Maritain, deserve the attention of anybody who claims to address modern politics.

The Christian Democratic movement in Europe and Latin America is arguably the most successful political movement of the twentieth century. One of its fruits, through the efforts of such Christian figures as Konrad Adenauer and Jean Monnet, is the European Union. Like the United Nations, the EU may be described as a good development, a bad development, or a good development that has gone off the rails. I tend to the third view, but, whatever the case, modern Christians who try to address the modern world should consider their example.

Further afield, rather than highlighting the efforts of those Christians outside of the political arena, why not address the contributions of Martin Lee, courageous and prudential leader of Hong Kong's democratic opposition? What of another Nobel Peace Prize winner, Kim Dae-Jung, the first real democratically elected leader of South Korea? I remember hearing him, on NPR no less, describing how, when the Korean CIA had him out on the ocean weighted with chains ready to throw him out a boat to drown, he prayed and had a vision of Jesus reassuring him that he would live, and then he heard the sound of American helicopters coming to his rescue.

---

16. John P. Humphrey, *Human Rights and the United Nations: A Great Adventure* (Dobbs Ferry, NY: Transnational Publishers, 1984), 65–66.

These examples could be multiplied from Africa, Asia, and Latin America. The contemporary world is full of thoughtful, courageous, Christian politicians deeply immersed in the life of politics itself. We may agree or disagree with their policies, but if we claim a universal faith, we cannot ignore their example.

CONCLUSION

Most politics is more like raising children than raising hell, more like gardening than grandstanding, more like work than warfare. Political action will not bring utopia. It will not conquer sin nor change human nature.

But it can make a difference between rampant crime and safe neighborhoods, between hungry families and economic security, between victory and defeat in war. And only those who have never been mugged, never been hungry, or never been at war, will think these differences trivial.

3

The Golden Triangle of Freedom

America's Sustainable Freedom and the Importance of Guarding It[1]

Os Guinness

I AM OFTEN ASKED why I speak so much about America as an Englishman, and I sometimes respond by telling the story of Winston Churchill, whom I remember meeting as a boy. He was once in Williamsburg being shown around by a very enthusiastic guide who suddenly stopped midsentence, realizing who it was she was talking to.

"Forgive me if it's embarrassing for you," she said, "for me to be introducing you to the town that was the cradle of the revolution against the English."

"Revolution against the English?" Churchill snorted, "It was an English revolution, led by Englishmen, with English ideas, fighting a German king and his German mercenaries." That is part of why I am such an admirer of this country and its great ideas and ideals. Many of them are English ideas that have come into their own in a fuller way than they did in England.

In 1843, a twenty-one-year-old Massachusetts scholar was doing research on the American Revolution and what led up to it. Among those he interviewed was Captain Levi Preston, a Yankee who was seventy years his senior and had fought at both Lexington and Concord.

---

1. This contribution was originally presented at the dedication of Pepperdine University School of Law's Herbert and Elinor Nootbaar Institute on Law, Religion, and Ethics, prior to Trinity Law School's "God and Governing" conference. It is included here with Pepperdine's permission.

> "Captain Preston, what made you go to the Concord fight?" was [my] opening question.
>
> The old man, bowed with the weight of fourscore years and ten, raised himself up-right, and turning to me, said: "What did I go for?"
>
> "Yes," I replied. "My histories all tell me you men of the Revolution took up arms against 'intolerable oppressions.' What was it?"
>
> "Oppressions? I didn't feel any that I know of."
>
> "Were you not oppressed by the Stamp Act?"
>
> "I never saw any stamps and I always understood that none were ever sold."
>
> "Well, what about the tea-tax?"
>
> "Tea-tax? I never drank a drop of the stuff: The boys threw it all overboard."
>
> "But I suppose you had been reading Harrington, Sidney, and Locke about the eternal principles of liberty."
>
> "I never heard of those men. The only books we had were the Bible, the Catechism, Watts's *Psalms and Hymns*, and the *Almanac*."
>
> "Well then, what was the matter, and what did you mean in going to the fight?"
>
> "Young man, what we meant in fighting the British was this: We always had been free, and we meant to be free always."[2]

Always free, free always—the daring of that thought deserves thought. Captain Preston was obviously very different from Founders such as James Madison, Thomas Jefferson, Alexander Hamilton, and George Washington. But he expressed with simple force what many of his generation dared to believe. It is surely the most daring philosophical and political theme of the entire Revolution—the conviction that you could create a free people who might remain free forever.

There is nothing more audacious in the entire American experiment than that. Yet though freedom is the glory of America, anyone who understands the history of freedom would have to say that freedom could also be the Achilles heel of America—unless Americans guard it in the way the Framers understood that it needed to be guarded. Allow me to sketch in some of the discussion surrounding this point. It may seem rather quaint

---

2. George Jones Varney, *The Story of Patriot's Day, Lexington and Concord, April 19, 1775: With Poems Brought Out on the First Observation of the Anniversary Holiday, and the Forms in Which It Was Celebrated* (Boston: Lee & Shepard, 1895), 170.

THE ESSENTIAL TASKS

to many Americans today, but for the Framers it turned on a deeply realistic understanding of history and how they sought to create a free republic that could remain free forever.

There are three essential tasks in establishing a free republic, two of which are obvious and the third often neglected:

The first task is to *win freedom*. Needless to say, that was the point of the Revolution—1776. But remember that the French achieved it too—1789, and the Russians also did—1917. That task is not unique to the United States, though no country celebrates and prizes its revolution as the U.S. does.

The second task was to *order freedom*. That was the purpose of the Constitution—1787. The French and the Russian revolutionaries did not manage that. Their revolutions spiraled down to demonic disorder and tyrannies that were worse than those they replaced. But the genius of your Founders is that they won freedom and they ordered freedom. They gave freedom a political, legal, and constitutional framework in which it could thrive.

The third task was to *sustain freedom*, and this is the part that is usually overlooked today. When Benjamin Franklin was asked what they had achieved as he came out of the Philadelphia Convention, he answered famously, "A republic, Madame, if you can keep it."[3] And that was more than the work of the few years that it took for the Revolution, or the thirteen years that it took for the Constitution. It was a task for decades and centuries, including our own day and beyond. There were later presidents, and some who were leaders before they were presidents, such as the young Lincoln, who talked about "the perpetuation of our free institutions."[4] Ironically, however, here we are in a day when we talk endlessly about such things as sustainable growth, sustainable development, and sustainable capitalism, but almost no one talks about sustainable freedom.

---

3. Michael P. Riccards, *A Republic, if You Can Keep It: The Foundation of the American Presidency, 1700–1800* (Westport, CT: Greenwood, 1987), 41.

4. William Henry Herndon, *Herndon's Life of Lincoln: The History and Personal Recollections of Abraham Lincoln* (Cambridge, MA: Da Capo, 1983), 152.

God and Governing

THE CLASSICAL MENACES

When the Framers talked about the tasks of freedom, they did so knowing why freedom was never easy, and why it is actually harder to be free than not to be free. The American Framers were revolutionary, but they were also rooted. They knew their history. In fact, you can say they used history in order to defy history. They had such an extensive understanding of the Greek and Roman classics that they were very aware of why freedom did not last, and what they would have to do to overcome the reasons why it did not.

One reason was the simple fact of external enemies. For the Framers, that was not a major problem. The United States was to be a continent-sized nation, with two huge oceans as a buffer, incredible human and natural resources, a weak and defenseless native population, and the nearest serious enemies three thousand miles away. That of course was then. With jet travel, intercontinental ballistic missiles, and the Internet, external enemies are a menace again—as September 11 reminds us so savagely.

The second and third menaces were much more important for the founders. The second is what the Greek historian Polybius called "the corruption of customs." What is decisive for a nation, he argues, is its constitution, its fundamental laws. Americans almost hear that and yawn. Is not the U.S. Constitution the world's oldest and best? But Polybius goes further. A constitution does not hang in the air. It rests on a bedding of customs, traditions, and moral standards. If this bedding is undermined, and the customs are corrupted, the best of constitutions will be subverted.

The last menace, in one word, is time. Or as Christians would say, nothing lasts because of the presence of sin and the passing of time. The Greeks and the Romans understood that with the passage of time, fresh things became formal, and things that are revolutionary became routine. Slowly, as Cicero warns, the vivid colors of the early republic fade away until what is left is easily distorted into becoming the Roman Empire. Time is not something we think about much today, though the young Lincoln warned about its effects as "the silent artillery of time."[5]

---

5. Donald Fehrenbacher, editor, *Abraham Lincoln: Speeches & Writings*, 1859–1865 (New York: Library of America, 1989), I:36.

The Golden Triangle of Freedom

THE FORGOTTEN BULWARK OF FREEDOM

The Framers were deeply conscious of each of these menaces, so their challenge was to create a free republic that could remain free despite them. How did they do it? If you ask most Americans today, they would answer that freedom is safeguarded in one way: the Constitution. That was in fact not the Framers' full answer. It was only half the answer, and the other half was equally important. They did not give it a name, but I call it "the golden triangle of freedom." This idea is so clear, bold, and constant throughout the Framers that it is amazing that it is not more discussed today.

The triangle goes like this: freedom requires virtue, which in turn requires faith, which in turn requires freedom (which in turn requires virtue, and so on, *ad infinitum*). Take the first leg of the triangle: freedom requires virtue. As Benjamin Franklin says, "Only a virtuous people are capable of freedom."[6] Virtue then requires faith of some sort. Beyond any doubt, the inspiration, content, and sanctions for virtue come from faith of some sort. And faith of any sort requires freedom. Therein lay the genius and uniqueness of the First Amendment religious liberty clauses. This golden triangle of freedom was to be the complement to the Constitution. Both were to act together to provide a safeguard so that the free republic might beat the odds and have a chance to last forever.

We are a long way in time and thought from the Framers, and much of our contemporary discussion of freedom is shallow compared with theirs. For example, many Americans today—including President George W. Bush—speak as if freedom were the sole political impulse and requirement of human beings, whereas the Framers knew that freedom had to go hand in hand with justice and order. Unless justice and order accompany freedom, all three will suffer.

Or again, many Americans today champion the notion that the highest freedom is negative freedom, or freedom from interference or imposition—the right to be let alone. Isaac Berlin, who was a great hero at Oxford when I was there, is famous for his distinction between the two themes of negative freedom, *freedom from interference*, and positive freedom, *freedom for excellence*, according to whatever vision you want

---

6. Benjamin Franklin to Abbés Chalut and Arnaud, April 17, 1787, quoted in Drew R. McCoy, *The Elusive Republic: Political Economy in Jeffersonian America* (Chapel Hill: University of North Carolina Press, 1980), 80.

to fill it with. In America today, many liberals, many young people, and all libertarians understand freedom only negatively; freedom is freedom from interference, freedom from imposition.

According to the Framers, the two sides of freedom needed each other. Freedom as independence from British colonialism was only half the story. The citizens of the new republic also had to be free to be citizens and therefore self-governing masters of their freedom—and for this they required the golden triangle of freedom. Negative freedom alone, particularly in its modern liberal and libertarian forms, would never have led to reforms such as abolition and the civil rights movement, and it would never guarantee that freedom will last.

Yet another contemporary conceit is that the only important freedom is external, or political freedom. Yet if you look over human history, particularly when you look at great faiths and philosophies, such as Buddhism, Stoicism, and the Christian faith, they put a high premium on starting with internal freedom. Stoics, for example, teach that the slave who is free internally is freer than his master who is distracted with all the cares of wealth. The American Revolution was obviously concerned with external, political freedom, rather than internal, spiritual freedom. But in the long run the external without the internal will not be robust, and it will not last.

Take the example of freedom and consumerism. We live in a day when freedom has become possibility and is equated with bare choice, of whatever kind. Our idea is choice, more choice, and choice of any sort, rather than right choice or wise choice. The result is endless consumerism, the betrayal of desire, and the accumulation of junk. In such a world internal freedom, including the freedom not to need endless choices and more and more junk, becomes a vital necessity for living humanly and guaranteeing external freedom, let alone a freedom that can last.

CONTEMPORARY MENACES TO FREEDOM

Two and one-third centuries after the Framers, we are in a generation when many have grown careless about the Framers' understanding of freedom and sustaining freedom. We therefore need to take account of contemporary menaces to American freedom. One menace is the widespread alienation of contemporary leaders from the ideas of the Framers. Significant sectors of the educated leadership in the country no longer believe in freedom as the Framers articulated it, and certainly not in sustaining freedom as the Framers saw it needed to be sustained.

For some people, this alienation is simply a matter of ignorance. They have never read what the Framers wrote. With others, it is a matter of carelessness. They have no interest. With yet others, it is more perverse. They hold views that are openly opposed to the Framers, to the original understanding of freedom, and to the original understanding of how freedom can be sustained. Their duty is to show what their alternative is and how it works better than the Framers' solution.

Another menace lies in the breakdown in the transmission of values. Jefferson and Tocqueville both understood that in a democracy every generation is a new people. Ideas and ideals therefore have to be handed on constantly in two ways. On the one hand, there has to be a reliable transmission from the older generation to the younger generation—we call that public education. American public schools were not just founded to be free universal education, but to teach the American virtues that provide the *unum* that balances and guards the *pluribus*, so that *E pluribus unum* remains an achievement as well as the national motto.

On the other hand, there has to be a reliable transmission from established citizens to new arrivals—in immigration. With all the talk on one side of "controlling of our borders" and on the other of "business growth," there has been a striking absence of talk about citizenship education. There is almost no limit to the number of people who can come into this country if they are educated as citizens when they arrive. But without citizenship education for those who come, even a few are a problem. One historian points out that it is relatively easy to become *an* American today, but increasingly difficult to know what it is to be *American*. The very notion of American identity and American citizenship has been seriously eroded.

The final contemporary menace—to use Polybius' term—is a corruption of customs. Anyone who follows the present culture wars will know how things that were self-evident and almost universally believed a generation ago—notions such as life, truth, the character of a family, and the importance of character in national leadership—are all deeply eroded or under vicious assault in some areas of this country. The question now arises whether future Americans will have the virtues needed to sustain freedom.

GOD AND GOVERNING

TOWARD A NEW, NEW BIRTH OF FREEDOM

Does this analysis leave me pessimistic? Not at all. It all depends on one's grounds for trusting in the possibility of national renewal. I have always been intrigued by the old understanding of the parallels between the Jewish, the Puritan, and the Framers' understanding of the projects they were each pursuing. First, there are parallels between how each of them understood their liberating moment—for the Jews *exodus*, for the Puritans *conversion*, and for the framers *revolution*. The ideas in each were different of course, but they also overlap.

Second, there are parallels between how each of them understood their constituting event: for both Jews and Puritans, through a *covenant*, and for the framers, through the *Constitution*.

Third, and this is the point usually overlooked, there are parallels between how they each understood that their projects might be renewed—for Jews, through a *return* to God's ways, for the Puritans through *revival*, and for the framers through what George Mason called "a frequent recurrence to fundamental first principles"[7] (or what Jefferson more daringly described as a revolution every twenty years).

Despite their differences, all three groups—along with the unanimous chorus of the ancients—were united in the recognition that no way of life, no political system, and certainly no freedom, can last forever. Not even the U.S. Constitution is a machine that would run on its own. Freedom has to be sustained over time, and the question is how.

You have all heard of the incomparable Alexis de Tocqueville. Toward the end of his life, the great champion of American democracy was increasingly disappointed by the outcome of the revolution in his beloved France. "In a [revolution], as in a novel," he observed, "the most difficult thing to invent is the ending."[8]

Your American Framers wrote a brilliant and daring, opening chapter to your epic national story, and at various crucial moments you have had the courageous leadership and the dedicated citizenry to sustain the greatness. Yet at this present moment of world dominance, you are experiencing a series of great crises. It would be wise to remember that, unless

---

7. Ben Perley Poore, editor, *The Federal and State Constitutions, Colonial Charters, and Other Organic Laws of the United States* (Washington, DC: govt. print off, 1878), 2:1909.

8. Alexis de Tocqueville, *Recollections: The French Revolution of 1848*, edited by J. P. Mayer and A. P. Kerr (New Brunswick: Transaction, 1986), 55.

The Golden Triangle of Freedom

there is national renewal, dominance will be followed by decline as surely as day is followed by night. The coming generation may well be the one to prove whether the Framers were right or wrong. Were they correct that freedom is never self-sustaining, and that it requires the strength of the Constitution and the strength of the golden triangle of freedom? Or have we matured beyond their worries, and can we continue to neglect their warnings with impunity?

If the Framers were right, you are living at an urgent moment. With your equal commitment to law and to faith, character, and virtue, your challenges and your tasks are clear. My hope and prayer will be that Trinity will be both a guardian and a guide to a better, wiser, more just, and a more free society—worthy both of your Framers' illustrious beginning and of the soaring majesty of the Jewish and Christian vision of law, freedom, justice, and human flourishing.

4

Lessons on Fleeing Temptation

Patrick Nolan

THE EVANGELICAL MOVEMENT POLITICS is at an interesting stage. We are questioning where we are heading, but that is healthy. It is important that we reconnect with where God wants us to go—there have been some stumbles along the way. It has been a movement long in making. Long before the Christian Coalition or Moral Majority, I was blessed to work with a fellow named Dr. Howard Kershner, who founded the Christian Freedom Foundation and published a newsletter called *Christian Economics*. His vision was to try to call the church into active involvement with public policy. Dr. Kershner died before he saw any fruit from his work as literally hundreds of preachers from across the country tried. But, eventually, the movement reached critical mass. We have had growing pains and, human as we are, we have made some mistakes along the way.

I used to teach horseback riding, and one of the things I learned is that as a horse runs, it stretches out its foreleg. However, before it can take another stride, it has to collect its legs underneath it, and in doing that it rebalances for the next stride. A horse can not run with its foot out all the time. It has to rebalance itself before it can stretch, and I think that this book initiates an attempt to rebalance Christian involvement in public policy. This has been a banquet for me intellectually. I have not been so inspired and had so much food for thought that will sustain a very long time. In the process of these discussions, God will reveal himself to us and show us where that next step will be.

I was the Republican leader for the California Assembly, and I had grown up in politics. I had been active in all of Reagan's campaigns, beginning at sixteen years old as the chairman of the Burbank Youth for Reagan when he first ran for governor. People forget that back then he was viewed as a wild extremist who had no chance. People laughed him off as a has-been actor and they did not see the core of his beliefs—those core principles that drove him. Many of the leaders of Youth for Reagan are still close friends. When we get together we remark on how fortunate we are to have been in on the ground floor of a movement that set out to change the country and ended up changing the world. We did not realize how blessed we were to have a leader like Ronald Reagan—whom we could believe in so completely and who would lead us forward with principle and with practical application of what he believed. People now say, "Which of the candidates is the next Reagan?" and I say "That's a fool's errand." A man like Reagan comes along not once in a lifetime, but once in a century! I would say he's of a caliber with George Washington and Abraham Lincoln at having transformed this country.

God uniquely prepared him for what he did. If you think about it, he led the Screen Actors Guild when the communists had their foothold in all the studios in Hollywood. He stood against them, and they threatened him because he challenged them—he and Jimmy Stewart, Bob Stack, the other lions of the industry, and they succeeded in taking back the Screen Actors Guild from the communists. The communists struck back. They threatened to throw acid in Ronald Reagan's face, and they threatened to kidnap his daughter Maureen. He understood the evil face of communism, and he understood when to fight them.

He also understood that there are also times to negotiate. He led the Screen Actors Guild in their first strike against the Hollywood studios. This put him in conflict with his boss at Warner Brothers Studio, Jack Warner, who also was the chief negotiator for all the studios. These tough negotiations taught him that it was important to know your bottom line, the essential things you have to walk away from with the negotiations.

Think of how God used the Hollywood strike to equip Ronald Reagan for his later negotiations with Mikhail Gorbachev at Reykjavik. The press and all the European elites were clamoring for Reagan to cut a deal with the Soviets to trade our missile defense in return for promises of peace. James Baker, Reagan's trusted advisor, was pressing him to deal away our missile defense. Even his wife Nancy implored him to make the deal. The future balance of power hung in the balance.

But Reagan knew the bottom line for the United States. The Soviets could not compete with the Star Wars missile defense. If he held that back, the Soviets would not be able to continue their aggressive policies. But if he had given that away, it would have brought him immediate acclaim as a peacemaker but it also would have allowed the Soviets to threaten the world with their bullying tactics. Reagan knew that he could not allow that to happen. Missile defense was our trump card and as long as we had that missile defense the Soviets would have to bankrupt their economy to try to neutralize it. In the end, they could not compete and they crumbled without a shot being fired.

But no one except Reagan believed that at the time. When he said no to Gorbachev's offer, the news broadcasts painted him as a villain and a warmonger. Reagan's wife, Jim Baker, George Schultz, the entire press corps said he was defeated there. But he knew he would live to negotiate again because he had the trump card. He understood his opponents. He had been fighting communism for decades. He knew what his hole card was, and he knew how to play the hand. More than a quarter of the world's population was freed from the dead hand of communist tyranny because of his fortitude. So God prepared him long beforehand for that struggle. I am unabashedly an admirer of Ronald Reagan.

I got elected to the legislature and tried to elect a Republican majority. Willie Brown was the Speaker and I was in California trying to do what Newt Gingrich did in Washington. We came within five votes of doing it, and then my office was raided by the FBI. They essentially accused me of taking a bribe, and for five years they investigated me. Every part of my life was a microscope. I supported the bill involved in the investigation because I believed in it. I would vote again for it today. But because the supporters of the bill contributed to my campaign, after I had voted for it several times, I was accused of racketeering. I said to my lawyer, "You know, I thought racketeering was to go after the mafia. Why are they coming after me?" and he said, "Well, you gotta understand that the mafia kidnaps prosecutors' children and shoots them, and you're no threat to them." The public was more than willing to believe that their representatives were corrupt, and in fact there were some that were. But I would be tarred with that same brush.

The investigation dragged on for over five years. I was emotionally exhausted and broke. They had worn me down.

Lessons on Fleeing Temptation

I faced a prison sentence of eight and a half years at a minimum, possibly twenty-one. My three children were at five years, four years, and ten months. I could not bear the thought of missing their entire childhoods. So when the prosecutors offered me a deal to serve thirty-three months, I bent to their will, and I lied and said I did something wrong. I accepted imprisonment for over two years in order to limit the damage to my family. That was difficult. I had given my whole life to trying to advance our conservative ideals and to elect a majority so that people could see what California would be like when governed by conservative principles. But God had a different plan for me.

I already had a strong faith when I went to prison. But God made himself so evident to me during my incarceration that I would say I went from believing in God, to knowing him.

My wife and I saw so many times that God's hand was on us during my incarceration. As difficult as it was, as painful as it was, we knew he was with us every step of the way. The day I was indicted, my wife and I walked out of my office to go to the governor's press conference room, where the press corps was waiting like lions in their den. On that very day my wife was due with our third child, our son. A secretary for another assemblyman stepped out from her office across the hall as we were walking toward the press conference room and pressed a note into my hand—she had written out by hand Jeremiah 29:11. At that very moment, being stripped of all I had worked for my life, I was given that message of hope: "'For I know the plans I have for you,' declares the LORD, 'plans to prosper you and not to harm you, plans to give you hope and a future.'"

The weekend before I went to prison, John Kurzweil, a dear friend who edits the *California Political Review*, drove with his wife and children seven hours up to visit Gail and me. We had a barbeque in the back yard, and in the course of the afternoon John said to me, "You know Pat, for centuries, Christians have left the day-to-day world, humbled themselves, prayed and studied their faith, done menial work, and we call that a monastery. View this time in prison as your monastic experience." How helpful to me was that message that this experience that would be so painful could be used to grow closer to God! I had gone to twelve years of Catholic school and was greatly blessed by the training I had had, but my preparation—my disciplines of the faith—had essentially stopped other than participation at church on Sunday. John's words that afternoon helped me go into prison with a positive focus. Here was a chance to reconnect and grow with God, to use this time—two years plus in prison—to grow closer to God.

As I surrendered at the prison, the normal practice would be for my counselor to walk me from the "big house," where you're stripped-searched and all the other ignominies, and into the labor camp that I was assigned to. But she was off that day, and instead it was just the guard on duty in the camp by rotation that was sent over for me. As I stepped through the three strands of barbed wire, he said, "Hello, I'm Officer Bernalzani." I said, "Hello, I'm Pat Nolan." And he replied, "Oh, I know who you are. My prayer group's been praying for you." Now we've all seen prison movies, and here I am a fat, old white guy going to prison. I did not know what to expect, and was frankly pretty fearful. But here was that reassurance from God, stepping into the unknown, that he was with me. Now there were seven hundred guards that worked in that pod of three prisons there. Of those seven hundred, Bernie was the only officer who would have prayed that way and been that explicit about his faith. Yet God appointed him to come and help me across into that unknown.

During the two years inside, God helped me think about my life and how I had lived my Christian faith. I did have a strong belief in God, but one of the things he really placed on me was Proverbs 3:5–6: "Trust in the LORD with all your heart, and do not lean on your own understanding. In all your ways acknowledge Him, and He will make your paths straight." I thought I trusted in him, but I learned I didn't really. I had hubris. I thought that because I came from a good family, had an excellent education, had a strong faith, and was in a position of authority, what I would do would be God's will. I forgot the most important thing: I should have asked him. It came to me so clearly that while I thought I trusted him, I really had not. I had relied on my own understanding instead of him.

Hopefully you will never go to prison, but I guarantee that you will have some crisis in your life that will shake you to your core. That is where your faith will sustain you. There will be an illness that confronts you or your spouse. It could be the death of a child, a bankruptcy—something that upends your life completely. That is when you will draw on your faith. That is when it will be tested. That is when God will reveal himself to you. C. S. Lewis said that we are God's sculptures. It is the chisel strokes that are so painful that he uses to make us his work of art. He will gouge deeply into you, and he will be forming you. If you submit to it, you will become his work of art and an instrument in sharing the joy with others. So I hope some of the lessons I have learned will be useful to you, not in the prison setting, but in whatever challenges that you face in your life.

The first thing is to look for God at work around you. I saw him so powerfully in prison. You know I mentioned Diana Card giving me Jeremiah 29:11, Bernie saying he'd been praying for me and John Kurtzweil telling me to use it as a monastic experience, but there were so many other times I saw God at work. Of course, he was acting around me my whole life—I was just oblivious to it. When I was in college one of my roommates was a master fly-fisher and I was a kid from central-city L.A. I did not know how to fly-fish and he took me up to Mammoth Mountain. He said, "Drop the fly right over there by those three fish that are going against the flow of the stream." Well, I looked over there and I could not see any fish. All I saw was the reflection of the mountains there. But over time as I looked I could see the fish slowly moving back and forth. Now, I was not able to drop the fly there, but I could see them. I thought so many times, that is the way God works. The fish were there all the time I just did not know how to look for them. Once you do, once you do look in and see God, it is amazing what he is doing all the time, to help us.

When I was in the legislature, I was from a district that was very pro-death, strongly pro-abortion. Planned Parenthood in Pasadena was at the apex of the social structure. I held a coffee at the home of a supporter in Pasadena and the leadership of Planned Parenthood packed the coffee with their supporters. From the very first question they pummeled me with attacks on my pro-life positions. I could not get my answer finished before the next attack was launched. I was like a fighter on the ropes—just being battered. Out of nowhere, this tiny little man stepped forward and said, "What you're talking about is killing babies." He confronted them with the evil that they were doing, and much like Dracula confronted with the crucifix held up, they melted away. That kind little man saved the day, literally.

I went up to him afterwards and said, "Sir, I don't know who you are and I don't know why you're here." And he said, "I don't know either. I was at the dinner table, and I saw the notice and said 'I need to go.'" And I said, "Well, God sent you. You literally rescued me and allowed me to talk about other things, and you spoke the truth." As I look back, I see so many times that God has been at work around me. So, I urge you look for him at work around you. You will be in awe of the things that he is doing.

The next thing I would say is be humble. Admit that you do not know everything. You do not have to know everything. In fact, I have found when you admit that, people are grateful, because they know nobody can know everything. Admit when you are wrong. It is so important that you acknowledge when you are wrong. I was on the prison-rape elimination commission and we had a very difficult conversation. A chair of the committee was a federal judge and he and I got into it a little on an issue, and our voices raised. I immediately wrote back and apologized. I have learned that you have to apologize right away.

Part of our witness is that, even if we think we are right, if someone else has been offended we have to say we're sorry. It is tough to say you're sorry, especially when you think you are right. In prison, on Thanksgiving Day, phone calls to your family are such treasures and there are so few phones for so many people. My wife was at her mother's house with our kids and she had to leave at a certain time in order to get home. If I did not get on the phone by a certain time I would not be able to talk to them. One of the guys, a gang member from L.A., was on the phone and he spent forty minutes, even though each call is supposed to be limited to fifteen minutes. After his overlong conversation, he hung up and dialed another number. One of the other guys said, "Hey! What are you doing?" and I said, "Hey, come on now, we've all got families we want to talk to." He yelled back at us and it raised quite a ruckus.

Everybody knew I was a Christian. So, my display of temper was a bad witness to the nonbelievers. I was mortified when the kid on the phone next to him turned and said, "Hey guys, I'm on the phone with my grandmother. Can't you hold it down?" I felt about two inches tall. Our families all worry about whether we are safe in prison and this youngster's grandmother heard the yelling in the background. I am sure she was worried.

I went back to my room and God said, "You've got to go apologize." And I said, "Uh-uh. I was right. He shouldn't have been making another phone call." And he said, "You've got to go apologize." I had this argument with God for about fifteen minutes. I finally gave in and went looking for the guy that I had argued with. I went up and said, "I'm sorry," and he said, "Hey man, that's okay."

I went up to Andre, the kid that had been on with his grandmother, and touched him on the arm—you know you are never supposed to touch anyone in prison. He turned on me and like he was about to punch me, but I was able to say, "Hey, Dre, I'm sorry—I shouldn't have done that." I saw the power of apology there. He just wilted in front of my eyes. Here this tough guy had probably never had anyone say they were sorry to him. He had to struggle for everything all his life, had to fight for everything. But he was so obviously touched by my apology. A simple apology can make a world of difference.

So part of humility is saying you are sorry even if you think you are right. If someone has been offended by us, we do not want to scandalize the church, we do not want to give a bad witness. We are responsible for our actions, even if we did not provoke them but we did not say "no." Saying "no" to your enemies is fun. Saying "no" to your friends is the tough part when they are intent on doing something you know is wrong. Saying to them, "I know you want to do this, I know you think it's right, but you shouldn't do it and here's why." That is very tough. It is easier just to shrug and let it go.

In the book *The Reivers*, William Faulkner tells of a grandfather who is talking to the son who has violated his trust: "A gentleman always accepts the responsibility of his actions and bears the burden of their consequences, even when he did not himself instigate them, but only acquiesced in them, didn't say 'no,' though he knew he should."[1] That is so important, though I would say "Christian" rather than "gentleman." Even though we do not instigate things, there are times we have to speak up and say "no." That is especially true for anyone that holds public office. You sometimes have to fight the team mentality in which wrongs are overlooked because pointing them out would harm the team. Unfortunately, the team mentality allows the lowest common denominator of conscience to rule. When there is somebody else that does not share our moral values that does something wrong, do you speak out or do you just acquiesce? Well that is what happened to the Republican majority in Congress. They began acquiescing to the least common moral denominator, and part of that is that we are not trusting in the Lord at that point. If we are acquiescing in order to be part of the team, we are not trusting in God to sustain us if we speak the truth to them. If we asked them not to do it, we should be relying on the Lord to touch their heart or in some way change things so that the team can still win. If you are for the right things, he wants you to win. We do not have to shave the truth, we do not have to shave morals to

---

1. William Faulkner, *The Reivers: A Reminiscence* (New York: Random House, 1962), 302.

win, but I have found that this is the toughest issue confronting Christian politicians. If you are ever in office, pray about that. Pray for the guidance to be able to speak to a friend and say "no," and try to restrain them from doing wrong.

One of the things I have learned is that God does not grade on the curve. Just because our opposition has cheated does not mean that we can. That is tough. It is tough because we want to play by the same rules, but we can not. We are held to a higher standard. Not Democrats and Republicans, but just people who do not have our values are willing to do that, and we have to just be held to that higher standard and be tougher on ourselves. In that is a great freedom, because I used to have to worry about pleasing 50 percent plus one. Now I just have to please one, and he is the constituency that counts. At the final judgment, he is not going to say, "What do the people at Glendale and Burbank think?" He'll say, "What did you do for me?"

Breaking God's heart is in essence what sin is. The right order of the world is what he wants. He wants peace and tranquility for us. When we sin, when we break that right order, when we lie or if we harm someone, it breaks his heart. It not only harms others, it harms our relationship with God and that is what we are held accountable for. One of the problems of modern society—and it especially expresses itself in our elected officials, who do reflect society—is the absence of the discussion of sin. One of the fellows I work with in Prison Fellowship, Jeff, was a court clerk in South Carolina and he padded his expense account to the extent of about $900. He was caught and he paid back three times, voluntarily. He said, "Look, I'm wrong. I did it." But the judge decided to make an example of him and sentenced him to two years in prison for $900.

While he was in prison they had a therapeutic circle group, and a graduate student said, "Well, tell us why you're in here." And when it came around to Jeff he said, "Well, I took something that wasn't mine. I sinned." And the leader said, "No, no, no. We don't talk about sin here. We don't mention that." And then she said, "Well, were you abused as a child? Were your parents alcoholics?" The irony is that Jeff's dad was a high official at Bob Jones University, so there clearly was no liquor; none of those issues. She was looking for an excuse for his behavior. Here he was admitting his sin, and yet she still wouldn't accept it.

That is one of the things our ministry brings into our prisons—holding people accountable, but with love. In prison they deny sin, but they often emotionally berate all the prisoners. I was yelled at, screamed at, humiliated; in two years I was probably told four or five thousand times, "You ain't got nothing coming." And it is said with malice. In essence that phrase means, "You're worthless. You come from nothing. You are nothing. You will be nothing." It is constantly repeated to you. On the other hand, Prison Fellowship's volunteers come in and say, "You're a child of God, created in his image with love. And no matter what you've done, I've sinned too and Jesus died for both of our sins. He made up for that. He's already forgiven you. Take him into your heart, and live by his precepts and you can live a glorious life forever with him in heaven." Now contrast those messages: "You are nothing, you come from nothing, you're worthless," versus "You're a child of God and you can live with him forever." We offer a message of hope to the prisoners—people that society would rather forget about. But Jesus didn't forget about them. He came for them, he came for us! We have all fallen short of the glory of God and that is the message we share with them.

As legislators, the problem is, of course, our pride. A priest once said to his congregation, "The center of sin is 'I.'" And, oh, he hit the nail on the head. It's "I." Think about original sin. What did the serpent say? "Ye can be as gods. You don't have to listen to God. You don't have to follow his ways. That's all clap trap. You! You can be your own god." And we succumb to that. We begin to think our ways are the right ways. We do not ask him. We do not submit. So, the next thing I would like to say is that we should submit completely. We cannot reserve a little part of ourselves for God. In my experience it cannot work that way. We cannot say, "Oh, I'll go along with God but I'm still going to control this one small part of my life." That does not leave room for God. It is not until you are flat on the floor, sucking the carpet fibers saying, "I can't handle this, I can't. I can't figure this out. I need you to help me." That is where there is room for God. When we totally surrender to him, then there is room for him to work.

When my children were young and still in the baby seat, sometimes they would reach out and grab the steering wheel. They wanted to help daddy drive. As they did that, with just that tiny little hand, it was almost impossible to drive. Just that little bit threw the whole balance off. That is a good analogy to how we work with God. He is driving along doing a great job and we think we are going to help Daddy. We grab that wheel and we think we are going to help drive our lives but we can not. If we grab the wheel we mess things up. Only by being totally sold out to him can he work his purposes through us.

He shows us the way. "Thy word is a lamp unto my feet." Think about what a lamp was then. In those days it was a little bowl, and when you lit the wick a tiny circle lit up. We stand there on the path and we wonder, "Where's God taking us? What's down there?" We want to have a flood light to light it all up for us. We would even be grateful for a flashlight. Instead, all he gives us is this lamp, his Word, and it lights up that little circle. We have a choice: we can stand there, fearful of where he is taking us, and nothing happens, or in faith we can step into that little circle. What happens then? The next step is lit up and he leads us where he wants us to go. He lights each step as we go along. We can not figure it out. We are not smart enough to figure it out. We can not think on all the levels he does. I love the hymn that reminds us, "Trust and obey . . . for there's no other way to be happy in Jesus." We have to trust and step into that circle of light. Even when we are frightened, even when we do not understand, even when it is painful, he will light our path.

I'm frustrated at times. Why can we not win? Then God reminds me that he is sovereign. Think about Dr. Bernard Nathanson, a man who aborted more babies than anyone in history. He made millions in profits off abortion clinics. He founded National Association for the Repeal of Abortion Laws (NARAL) to help advance abortion. Then one day he was beginning an abortion, and on the sonogram he saw the baby reach for the needle and he stopped. He stopped that abortion, and he stopped all his abortions. He realized this was a child and he began studying the Word of God. He abandoned all his clinics and his whole program and began studying. He converted and was baptized.

Charles Colson put that into context. He said, "Standing there, watching Dr. Bernard Nathanson being baptized, giving his life to Christ, I realized that God is sovereign." Satan and his army can win all the battles politically. They can win elections, they can win court decisions, they can win people over to their side, but in one millisecond God can touch the heart of even the most hardened sinner. We do not choose the time and place of victory; all God calls us to is obedience. We are called to be faithful, not successful. We may never see success in life, but we know he will win. That is trust, and without trust we fall prey to doing things our own way and it is never his way. We have to faithfully do what he calls us to do with confidence and rely on him to choose the time and place of success.

Lessons on Fleeing Temptation

There are also times when there is just so much to do. When John Von Kannon of the Heritage Foundation heard what I was doing he said, "Well, I get it. Prison Fellowship saves souls retail and Justice Fellowship saves souls wholesale." We work on the laws and policy, and I easily get frustrated when I focus on all the work to be done with only myself and my assistant to do it. I tell people it is like the Wizard of Oz. We are the little man behind the curtain and we are trying to effect laws in all fifty states. It is overwhelming at times. Then I remember that when I was in prison my sister sent me a prayer written by Alexander Solzhenitsyn, and the last two lines are so helpful. Whenever you are burdened, thinking about how are you going to accomplish something or even how God is going to accomplish it, think about these lines. Solzhenitsyn prayed, "I look back in wonderment at the journeys beyond hope—to this place, from which I was able to send mankind a reflection of your rays. And however long the time that I must now reflect them, you will give it to me. And whatever I fail to accomplish you surely have allotted unto others."[2] God's got it covered. He does not expect the impossible of us. He only expects us to do what he has asked us to do, and if we faithfully do it, we should then have the confidence to leave it to him to assign the tasks to someone else, knowing that he knows how he is going to win the victory and with whom.

That lifts such a burden from me. I keep on my desk a plaque that says, from Psalm 46:10, "Be still and know that I am God." There are times when I am so uptight I can hardly figure how to do what needs to be done, and I look over at that plaque, and it reminds me to "Be still and know that I am God." Just let him take it. My grandmother used to say, "Let go and let God," and I see now how wise that was. As I said before, all we have to do is trust and obey, and if we do that, we can then be a pencil in his hand, writing a love letter to the world.

---

2. Edward E. Ericson Jr. and Daniel J. Mahoney, editors, *The Solzhenitsyn Reader: New and Essential Writings, 1947–2005* (Wilmington, DE: ISI Books, 2006), 625.

5

The Future of Virtue and Statesmanship in Pagan America

Vishal Mangalwadi

THE CONFERENCE THAT LED to this book on virtue, ethics, and statesmanship is inconceivable in a law college in India. You don't associate lawyers with virtue and ethics. So far in this book we have looked at American history to understand the present moment. I think it would be appropriate to look forward at the challenges that the future will bring before us in the area of ethics and virtue and statesmanship. There are many institutions—the university, the press, the publishing, the entertainment, Hollywood, the church—that are shaping the culture. The church has been aching to capture Washington, but if the battle remains focused on Washington, then even an electoral victory or two could actually mean losing the culture.

Let's begin with one of my scripts for Hollywood: tentatively, it is called *2048*. That's year 2048. America has become pagan and totalitarian. China has become Christian and free. A Caucasian family of scientists in Washington, D.C., is fighting a high-tech battle for liberty. The wife has already been kidnapped for leading a campaign against the law that requires her father-in-law, a retired scientist, to die. His "right to die" has become his duty to die because he is considered too old, too senile to live. He is too much of a burden on society considering that the economy is in trouble. So, she resists the law and is kidnapped. Because of her value as a scientist, she is not killed immediately. The White House wants her to reform her ways and fall in line, but her little children, a twelve- and thirteen-year-old boy and girl, initiate the battle to liberate her. Soon, the whole family gets involved in the conflict—the dog, the father, and some relatives. The family's high-tech battle for liberty in Washington, D.C., is orchestrated by the "senile," "bed-ridden," "dying" grandfather and is supported by an underground Chinese church that exists in Washington in the guise of a software company.

This scenario is not imaginary, as many of you already know that secular humanism is an unstable worldview. It stands on Christian foundations which it seeks to destroy. Many secular thinkers, especially in what used to be called the "New Age," know that without Christian foundations secularism has to give way to another idea. At this moment, paganism appears to be the strongest contender as America's future, or at least as your children's future. Therefore, targeting that generation, this action-film script explores the relationship of paganism to totalitarianism and of Christianity to freedom. Secular education has misled Americans into believing the foolish idea that freedom is an automatic product of "common sense." The film will teach that common sense and freedom will disappear from America because what was called common sense by people such as Thomas Paine was a *myth* created by the Scottish Enlightenment, and that freedom is a fragile flower that blossoms only in certain mature cultures. Pagans want freedom but paganism cannot sustain freedom.

But is Paganism America's future?

A few years ago, I was speaking in St. Olaf College in Minnesota, which is a Lutheran college. After the lecture I was going for lunch. Some young women students were selling Durga Frisbees. Durga is the Hindu goddess of Shakti, or power. That is, tantric power, sexual power, or supernatural power derived from sexual energy and demons. As I looked at those young women, I said to myself that a few years ago they would have been selling Frisbees with pictures of Marilyn Monroe, and a generation before that they would have been selling Frisbees with Scripture verses on them. Now they are selling Frisbees with this goddess of tantric sexuality. What next? Well, within a couple of years a Hindu professor became the chair of the Religion Department. He is still there.

That's just one indication of America's march towards paganism. Note these statistics:

- In 1997, MTV surveyed 14–25-year-old young people about what was the most important thing they wanted to learn about. The top answer was "Tantric Sex."[1]
- Tantra.com has reported getting 50,000 hits per day.[2]
- *The Da Vinci Code*, which assumes that the Lord's Supper was a ritual practicing tantric sex or gnostic sex, has already sold more than 70 million copies.[3]

What does it mean to live in a pagan culture? What does a quest for ethics and virtue mean in a pagan setting?

A simple way to answer that question would be tell you my own story of moving out of secular India into pagan—animistic—India. Ruth and I were married in 1975, and in January of the following year we moved to a farm outside a village in a very backward area, where tantric sex used to be the state religion a few centuries ago. The most explicit, erotic temples are in that area just fifteen miles from where we were living and working.

About a year after we moved there we noticed that two or three times a day, about a third of a mile from our home on the main road, motorcycles would stop with two guys sitting on them with rifles on their backs. They would talk to our neighbors. We didn't know what was going on but we assumed that they were curious about us. That was understandable—young couples from cities do not come to live in poor villages that offer no job opportunities, no telephone, television, running water, or security. But it was not curiosity that was driving these gun-toting motorcyclists. Our neighbors whispered to us that they belonged to Ram Singh's gang, and they were planning to attack us. We were on an isolated farm about five miles outside the city and about a mile outside the village.

We lived on the farm partly because we understood that our area was so poor and backward because the peasant farmers did not live out on the farms. Why? Because it was far too insecure. They had to live in small huddled villages next too each other. If you live out on the farm you can grow vegetables or fruit. Just developing fruit orchards in that

---

1. "About Tantra Works," Enoughism, online: http://www.enoughism.org/about_tantra_works.htm.

2. Ibid.

3 "'Da Vinci Code' follow-up in works," *The Hollywood Reporter*, April 20, 2009, online: http://www.hollywoodreporter.com/hr/content_display/film/news/e3if26a27fe344b20e4695aa0b11fdab1b4.

part of India could turn our region into an economy like that of parts of fruit-producing California. The soil is good, the weather is great. The problem is that no one plants fruit because you cannot protect the fruit you grow. If you do not live on a farm, you cannot have biogas, you cannot have poultry. And why can you not live outside the village on your farm? Because it is far too insecure.

Why is it so insecure? If you have even one fruit tree, the upper caste men from the village will come and take your fruit. If you protest, they will rape your wife and your daughter. It is a culture built on relativism, where the law "Thou shalt not covet thy neighbor's vineyard" was never taught. It is a culture without "Thou shalt not covet," "Thou shalt not steal," or "Thou shalt not rape or commit adultery." This idea that there are moral absolutes that are binding on all people is not a part of pagan culture. Perhaps I should not generalize so much. Relativism means, "Yes, *you* should not rape, *you* should not covet, *you* should not steal, but I am higher caste; those rules don't apply to *me*." That is the pagan relativist mindset. Morality is meant to bind *you*, not *me*.

So, I heard these reports that these motorcyclists belonged to this dreaded gang. The father of this gang leader had lived as a *dacoit*—an armed gang of bandits—for thirty years. The police had not been able to arrest him. When he was old he surrendered to a Gandhian leader, but his gang did not disappear. The younger members of the gang regrouped around his son and metamorphosed into an urban gang. The son, Ram Singh, became the biggest gangster in the city. Our neighbors said that this gang was planning to attack me. What was I to do? I prayed, consulted some friends, and finally decided that it would be unwise to face a dozen or a half dozen armed robbers after they had already entered my home, where it was just me and my wife. It would be much better to go into their den and confront the leader there.

Ram Singh had taken over two rooms in a hotel permanently and didn't pay for them. His gang ate from all the restaurants and no one ever asked them to pay for anything. When I went to them, their room was full of smoke, full of alcohol, and he was pouring whiskey for himself. Two guards with rifles were standing at the door.

They asked me, "Who are you?"

"I'm Vishal Mangalwadi," I said to them, "from Gatheora village. I want to see Ram Singh."

"About what?" they yelled. But I didn't have to answer because he came towards me and bowed down very politely saying, "I'm Ram Singh. What can I do for you?"

I said, "I hear you're planning to attack me, so I've come here to save you the trouble of coming to our village. I want to know what is your problem, and if we can sort it out."

Ram Singh was stunned.

He mumbled, "How can I do such a wicked thing? I hear so many good things about what you are doing for the poor people. I've no plan of attacking you. It's the other gang of the MR that's active in your area. They may be scouting around to plan an attack on you." (I will not write MR's full name because he graduated from being a gangster to winning a democratic election in our area, and still wields a lot of power.)

Ram Singh went on: "It's MR's gang that is planning to attack you. But this is ridiculous. He is robbing and looting and then he takes my name—saying that I'm doing it. I'm getting a bad reputation."

He then turned to two of his men and ordered them to get on a motorbike, go to MR at once, and tell him that he must leave "these good people" alone. If he didn't, he would have a real fight on his hands this time.

I couldn't believe what was happening. The two guys flung their rifles on their shoulders, kick-started their motorbike, and off they went. Ram Singh invited me to join him for a drink. I felt uncomfortable in that setting. He sensed that I didn't belong in that room, so he said that I must come to his home to dine, and he let me go.

Ruth and I felt safe, but what we didn't realize was that, in an attempt to help us, Ram Singh had actually turned a gangster against us who was to become more powerful than him. He fought the next election to the state parliament, won it, and became our political leader. Then he controlled the district administration and the district police. Today, our most competent young people go into private-sector industry and business; back then, during the socialist phase of our economy, the competent people took up jobs with the government. The "civil servants" were the most educated products of the secular humanist university system. (Incidentally, William Wilberforce's Clapham Sect and outstanding Christians such as Lord Macaulay had played key roles in building up India's administrative infrastructure. Back then, our civil servants had good appearance. They

The Future of Virtue and Statesmanship in Pagan America

were university graduates and savvy. Everyone who saw them from a distance thought of them as good and sophisticated lot.)

These "sophisticated" men and women educated in British secular system—rather than real Pagan Indians—were ruling over us and we were very pleased about it. However, to make a long story short, soon I was to see what paganism had done to our secular elite. One afternoon a hail storm struck our district, flattening the wheat harvest and shattering the handmade tiles that covered the thatched roofs of the poor in hundreds of villages. There was much wailing, so I knelt down and prayed that the Lord will help us bring some relief to them. The very next day a gentleman came and visited me from Delhi. He said, "I work for EFICOR—the Evangelical Fellowship of India Commission on Relief. I was passing through this region and decided to see these world famous [erotic] temples. I've been reading reviews of your book on the Gurus. Since I was in the area I decided to come and see you, because many people in Delhi are talking about you that you've left the city and you are here in the village serving the poor people."

I started telling him about the tremendous damage that the hail storm had done the previous day. He said, "Actually, I just stepped out of the bus when the hail storm hit, so I saw it first hand. I would like to help you do some relief work through my organization." So, we notified the local tabloid press that we were planning to give some relief to the victims of the hail storm. We wanted peasant farmers to come and submit their applications for relief, and then our team would visit them, survey the damage, and determine what we could do for them.

By the time we notified the press, three or four days had gone by since the storm. None of politicians had used the "R" word—relief. Government had done nothing, politicians had said nothing. So the press was very excited, the tabloids made it the front-page headline: here's a bunch of Christian young people who are offering relief for the poor in our district, implying that our elected and highly paid leaders are indifferent to even the greatest tragedy of the moment.

The press got the peasants excited. That infuriated the gangster-turned-politician, and he pressed upon the district magistrate (who was also the district collector—that is, both the revenue and the judicial officer) to send me a notice that our relief work was illegal. Allow me to interrupt the story to connect the dots between ethics, virtue, statesmanship, and governance to paganism and non-biblical cultures. I am using this real life story to help you understand why countries such as Iraq, Afghanistan, and Pakistan, where you are spending billions of dollars everyday, are not particularly excited about democracy. I'm also demolishing the myth that some universal "common sense" can sustain just, democratic governance. Why would a democratically elected politician oppose social work—relief for the victims of a hail storm? Why would a secular, university-educated judicial and revenue officer do the bidding of a criminal politician? What does democratic governance mean in such cultural settings?

When warlords and criminals become democratically elected politicians, they don't have to go out and rob individuals. They control the government treasury. So, to continue with my story, I received this notice from this highly educated district magistrate that my relief work was illegal, because there was a law in our state that in the event of a natural calamity no private party is allowed to collect donations without the permission of the state government. I wrote back a polite, formal response saying, "Thank you for telling me about this law. Since there is no time to get the required permission (and since the permission may never be granted), we will obey the law and not collect any donations. We will only give out relief."

Prompt came the second note: "If you're not collecting donations, how can you possibly give out money? Your relief work is illegal, so it is banned."

I gave a second polite and formal response, saying that as good, Bible-obeying Christians we would obey the order of the magistrate. We would cancel the relief work, but we would organize a prayer meeting. We will simply ask the peasants to pray and ask God to grant them relief. Our prayer meeting will not be sectarian. It will be open to all communities. Therefore, it will not be held in a church but in the Gandhi ashram. This will make it possible for people of all faiths to come together in a Gandhian style prayer meeting.

The magistrate was a hardworking, disciplined bureaucrat. Promptly, he sent me a third notice, written and delivered at night: "Your prayer meeting will disturb the law and order and peace and tranquility of the district, therefore, your prayer meeting is hereby banned."

At that point we had to make a hard theological decision: Did the word of God require us to obey this order or did the Bible require us to disobey his order?

The Future of Virtue and Statesmanship in Pagan America

The government's stance helped us begin to understand why our people were so poor. It helped me begin to understand something more of what Jesus meant by the "Kingdom of God."

When was Jesus moving around in Galilee, people were brought to him who were paralyzed, blind, sick, and demon-possessed. In my pagan culture, a religious leader would look at a paralyzed man and say, "This is his karma." The "common sense" of Muslim folk culture would say, "This is his fate." People may feel sorry for the paralyzed man. Or they may say, "This is God's curse"—or "this is God's will" (*inshe Allah*). But Jesus didn't accept those physical, mental, social, spiritual evils as God's will. He proceeded to change the reality around him—to heal the sick and deliver the demonized. For Jesus believed that God's will was abundant life for the people he had created in his own image, the people that he loved and wanted to have as his beloved children. So as crowds gathered around Jesus, he sat down on a mountain and began to declare, "Blessed are the poor in spirit, for theirs is the Kingdom of God."

Here were people who, as Jews, saw themselves as under a curse; as people who were wretched, not blessed. But Jesus was declaring that the Kingdom of God had come to turn the wretched of this world into the blessed of God. That is what seeking justice means: they were not supposed to be poor, they were supposed to be living in a land flowing with milk and honey—and once it did. But now they were poor, because they lived in a Bible belt that had been taken over by pagan Rome. They were living under paganism and they were feeling the consequences.

They knew a God who acted in history to break every chain, every yoke; to set free the captives, the oppressed. This is the God who demands that we love justice, act justly, seek justice, love mercy, and walk humbly with him. He cares for those who are mourning, those who are sorrowing, and those who are hungry and thirsty.

Jesus saw the crowds as sheep without a shepherd. Well, they had Herods, and Pilates, and chief priests—just as we have our democratic and bureaucratic leaders—but their Jewish and Roman leaders had turned into wolves. Jesus was initiating a subversive movement. He was calling the sheep to follow him so that he may turn them into shepherds—those who would govern under God. That's Jesus's language for what statesmanship or leadership is all about. He's ushering in a new kingdom—a revolution, if you prefer modern terminology—that takes sheep and turns them into shepherds.

What is Jesus seeking to accomplish? He says he is starting a new kingdom, the Kingdom of God. He is bringing to an end the present kingdom of Satan, the kingdom of evil, the kingdom of wolves, the kingdom of darkness. He is transforming this world of the wretched into a kingdom of the blessed—the Kingdom of God. That is why he asked his disciples to pray, "Thy kingdom come, Thy will be done on earth." Jesus believes in the sovereignty of God, but he does not believe that what is happening right now is God's will. The misery around him is Satan's will. It needs to be transformed. It needs to be challenged.

What does paganism mean—this worldview that is overtaking the Bible Belt, that is, America? Paul tells us in Romans 1 that when the people exchange the truth of God for a lie, the first area of confusion and corruption is the area of sexuality. But it doesn't stop there, it corrupts the whole of society.

Last year my wife and I spent two weeks over Christmas with Mahatma Gandhi's grandson studying the Sermon on the Mount. He had joined our group of Indian writers with his wife. Both of them are scientists with PhDs from MIT in Boston. We were doing this because Mahatma Gandhi's vision for India, which he had described as *Ramrajya*, was substantially taken from the Sermon on the Mount. Just as manay Christians living in a Muslim culture use the term *Allah* to refer to God, Gandhi used the term *Ramrajya* to refer, not to the kingdom of the Hindu deity Ram, but to what (Gandhi thought) Jesus meant by the "Kingdom of God."

Studying the Sermon on the Mount with Mahatma Gandhi's grandson began to help us look at our nation—and the questions of ethics, virtue, and governance—from the perspective of the Sermon. We began to discuss the beatitudes, such as "Blessed are those who hunger and thirst for righteousness, for they shall be satisfied." What does it mean to hunger and thirst after righteousness and justice? I suggested that this was one area where Gandhi was not following the Sermon on the Mount. He was trying to establish his own righteousness.

For example, Gandhi's vow of celibacy was an attempt to become God. The term translated celibacy is *Bramacharya*. It is an attempt to harness the sexual energy to become *Brama*—God. How was Gandhi doing it?

Brahmacharya is translated as celibacy because the first step involves not dissipating your sexual energy through ejaculation. You train yourself to awaken the sexual energy but absorb it and bring it to your *crown-*

chakra, in your head. That gives you the psychic experience of ecstasy and realizing your own divinity. One result of this study was that I also began to look at Mahatma Gandhi's life. I found that Mahatma Gandhi was using many women to awaken his sexual energy—the names of at least ten such women are public knowledge. He required some of these women to "sleep" with him naked; this was a part of his understanding of "celibacy" or *Brahmacharya.*

One of the stories was most baffling for me. Mahatma Gandhi's second cousin was Kanu, whose wife was Abha. Gandhi insisted that Abha sleep with him naked. After a while his cousin Kanu offered to sleep with the Mahatma as his "bed warmer." But Gandhi said no: his *Bramacharya* ("celibacy") demanded that he sleep with young women. (The most charitable interpretation is that Gandhi honestly felt that he needed young women to awaken his sexual energy, which he could then use to gain the mystical experience and power of his inherent divinity.)

Most of Gandhi's biographers and commentators have hidden or explained away these *apparently* dark aspects of Gandhi's public life. In some versions of tantra, the yogi (practitioner) actually ejaculates and then through tantric "magic" tries to suck back the mixture of male and female fluid into his body and head to acquire the power to become god. All the details of what Mahatma Gandhi was actually trying to do in these "experiments" (his term) is not public yet. What we do know is this: after India's independence in 1947, Hindis, Muslims, and Sikhs started killing each other. About a million people were killed and ten million became homeless. Mahatma Gandhi said to the Congress Working Committee (Congress is a political party in India) that this mass madness was not the fault of the Hindus or the Muslims, but his fault for having "failed in my *Bramacharya*" (celibacy to achieve divinity). He meant that he had failed to become god, to realize his divinity, so that he could have the spiritual power to control these Hindus and Muslims and Sikhs.

In case you are lost by these disjointed, X-rated stories, let me connect the dots again between biblical and pagan worldviews and the meaning of ethics, virtue, and statesmanship. These terms have different meanings in different worldviews. In a pagan America, leadership and governance will mean something very different than what they meant in a Christian or secular (i.e., semi-Christian) America. One result of India's pagan cultural understanding of sex, marriage, celibacy, ethics, etc. was that it took over seventy years (from the 1870s to 1956) to outlaw polygamy. And yet, even in mid-1990s, we had at least one member of parliament who had forty-nine wives—and he didn't even know all of their names! Right now we have two female chief ministers who won their positions of leadership because they were mistresses of popular politicians.

What does that have to do with you? Well, your move towards paganism means that soon it will not be Hillary Clinton, but Monica Lewinsky who'll be running for the presidency of America. Does that matter?

A hundred years ago, missionaries came to India to rescue temple prostitutes (*deodasis*, now called "goddesses") from our pagan temples. Now (formerly) Christian colleges are encouraging young women in America to become goddesses by exploring their sexual energy! If the Internet is any guide, then there may be more temple prostitutes (called "temple goddesses") in California than in India! When you exchange the truth of God for a lie, your thinking becomes futile. The mind—and the colleges and universities—become darkened. This darkness may manifest itself in the area of sexual perversion first, but it doesn't stop there. Its understanding of ethics and virtue corrupts national heroes as great as Mahatma Gandhi, and in day-to-day life it makes a mess of democracy and justice. It becomes oppressive for the poor—the kingdom of Satan.

By the way, I refused to cancel that prayer meeting. The district superintendant of police called me to his home, sat me down in an easy chair, offered me tea and snacks, and told me he was reading my book. He had read the newspaper reviews of my book in the national press, and told me that he respected me as a celebrity and that I was jewel of the district, etc. "Nevertheless," he went on, "if you don't cancel the prayer meeting, I would kill you myself." The superintendent of police, who had sworn to uphold the Constitution of India, which guarantees my "fundamental right" to life and "freedom of religion," took two hours explaining to me in great detail how many public figures he had killed.

Why was he threatening to kill me for organizing a public prayer meeting for the victims of a hail storm? What do ethics, virtue, and leadership mean in a secular, democratic India—for a university-educated officer of the government of India? Participation in financial corruption such as bribery had put officers like him in a compromised position. He had to listen to a corrupt gangster-turned-politician who hated me. The highest police officer in my district was, in effect, telling me that the gangster wouldn't need to send a bunch of outlaws to kill me. He had acquired democratic power to tell the police officer to kill me if I didn't do his bidding.

What is the relationship of paganism to totalitarianism? In a pagan culture, what does it mean to pursue ethics, virtue, and statesmanship? For a non-governmental activist such as me, what does it mean to practice compassion for the victims of a natural calamity, or to seek justice when they are being denied service?

Well, if America's march towards paganism continues, then you will need to have John-the-Baptist figures to tell your Herod (in the White House or in a governor's mansion) that it is not right for him to be living with his brother's wife, multiple wives, or same-sex partners. When Paul was going out preaching in his pagan world, there were temples with as many as a thousand temple prostitutes. They would have been doing more than selling Durga Frisbees. According to today's professors of religious studies, this bigoted preacher, Paul, was an enslaver of women, but back then the goddess-worshipping women flocked to him. Pagan women found his message liberating.

To conclude, perhaps abruptly: In pagan America, you will not have the opportunity to be a statesman. You will have to become a prophet like John the Baptist and risk your head in pursuit of virtue and ethics, in your battle for culture, for Hollywood, for the soul of your youth in your schools and colleges.

6

The Failure of Evangelical Political Involvement

Dallas Willard

THE HEART OF THE question before us is quite simple: Why after 25–30 years of evangelical political involvement, with a high level of visibility and influence, is there little or no improvement in the ethical quality of American political discourse and practice? I'm not going to question the assumption that there hasn't been any improvement, as it seems to me that it is obvious. The words "integrity" and "maturity" were used in my assignment, and those are good words, but they don't cut very deeply today without some explanation. Integrity becomes an issue in public life, of course, as does maturity, but you need to spell out what they mean. And in this context to have maturity means that you have grown up ethically. It means that the ideals that are honored in discourse about the ethical or the moral life have increasingly come into your possession. Integrity would mean, among other things, that you don't have to run different processes in your life—that you're transparent and all parts of who you are consistently hang together, so you don't have to keep parts of yourself hidden. You don't live in the dark. But when you speak about growing up morally you are also actually talking about the ability to lead on important matters of life.

I so appreciated David Wells's discussion of debt. Debt is a primary problem for life, as is repeatedly emphasized in all "wisdom literature." "The borrower becomes the lender's slave" (Prov 22:7). Debt, if not handled with the utmost caution, undercuts the ability to live and to lead. It becomes a great destructive force. The greatest threat to the indispensable virtue of prudence in America is the credit card and easy credit: the ability to gain possession of things without paying for them. It is equally harmful at the level of government. John Maynard Keynes is mainly the one who brought deficit financing into respectable governmental practice. Some used to object to him that sooner or later you'd have to pay off the debt, and his brilliant reply was, "In the long run we are all dead."[1] Of course, after that *you* don't have to pay your debts; someone else does. Debt is a relentless burden, rarely well handled, though those who *sell* it to you present it as a wonderful opportunity. It is a constant threat to well-being and character, to maturity and integrity.

I want to address this question of the recent failure of Evangelical involvement in politics as directly as I can, by way of three related factors:

- *The lack of connection between the evangelical "gospel" at present and character development.* The fundamental message that is heard now from evangelicals is not what we have always heard from evangelicals and other Christians. Evangelical Christians have a long history, and pre-WWII evangelicalism, especially in the eighteenth and the early nineteenth centuries, was, quite simply, a different kind of religion—with very different practices and theological assumptions. *The disappearance of moral knowledge from the institutions of knowledge in our society.* The institutions of knowledge are primarily the universities, including higher education generally, and the church. You may find it strange to hear the church listed as an institution of knowledge, but if you do, that is precisely a part of our problem, and we have to deal with it.

- *The general withering of professional ethos.* Following upon the previous points, the professional's life is no longer tied to an exalted vision of dignity and public good.

THE EVANGELICAL "GOSPEL" AND THE LACK OF CHARACTER DEVELOPMENT

The current Evangelical understanding of salvation has no essential connection with a life morally transformed beyond the ordinary. Evangelicals are good at what they call "conversion." They're not good at what comes later, because *what is preached by them as the gospel has no necessary connection to character transformation.* Post-WWII evangelicalism is,

---

1. John Maynard Keynes, *A Tract on Monetary Reform* (Amherst, NY: Prometheus, 2000), 80.

basically, fundamentalism in doctrine minus the pugnacious attitude. Unfortunately, fundamentalism defined itself in terms of correct belief, but not in terms of practice. Correct beliefs were a big and important issue, and still are. I do not question that. But now we must understand that we have developed a doctrine and an understanding of belief that does not entail action. It is psychologically false, and biblically false in terms of the language that is used, but that is just the way evangelicalism has developed. "Saving faith" has no necessary implication for becoming Christlike. The idea of Jesus as Teacher, Master and so on, became code language among liberals in the pre-WWII era for "merely human." So if you talked about Jesus as Teacher, that meant you were dismissing him as divine Lord, so "Teacher" disappeared from the fundamentalist (and then the evangelical) vernacular. And, of course, where you do not have teachers you cannot have students. So discipleship gradually disappeared during the twentieth century. Discipleship has historically been the process of association with Jesus and his people in which you become like him. That disappeared from evangelical practice.

Now there are tons and tons of problems with this. This view is founded on a whole hermeneutic that set aside the Gospels and said that our gospel for today is Paul's gospel, which was different from what Jesus preached. The upshot is that now we have this lovely little bumper sticker: "Christians aren't perfect, just forgiven." The former is fine, the latter is not. Christians aren't perfect. The focus on perfection distracts from the real issue—character transformation and obedience—and we've avoided obedience long enough to no longer know how to obey. We have adopted this position under a misreading of the gospel among evangelicals that says, "Just forgiven." That's it.

How do we grow in Christlikeness? What does it look like? I will give a couple verses here just as illustrations of where such growth comes out. "Do nothing from selfishness or empty conceit, but with humility of mind regard one another as more important than yourselves" (Phil 2:3). Now just think of the effects of that, and of what it would be like to learn it to the point where doing it is easy—where it is not a strain but is an expression of who you really are—easy for you habitually to see others as better than yourself. Further on in that same chapter: "Do all things without grumbling or disputing; so that you will prove yourselves to be blameless and innocent, children of God above reproach in the midst of a crooked and perverse generation, among whom you appear as lights in the world" (Phil 2:14–15). That is basic Christian life from Paul's point of view. That is a life that wins the world and provides a model of life under God. That is a life that has to explain its source to an inquiring public, because it stands out and is so different. That is the New Testament vision. We are talking about taking 1 Corinthians 13, and saying, "Yes that's for me. I will do that. I will let love dwell in me to the extent that, because love dwells in me, I suffer long and am kind. Love also does not envy, does not puff itself up, does not exalt itself and so on." That would become my natural character. But in the evangelical gospel preached today there is no natural connection between what is preached as the gospel and the Christlikeness described in these verses.

There are three "gospels" heard today. The first is that believing Jesus suffered for your sins brings forgiveness and heaven. That is the standard version of the gospel among evangelicals. Is it true? Yes, it is true, but that is not the gospel. It is actually one theory of the atonement, and it does not make up the whole of the gospel. Did Jesus die for our sins? Yes, he certainly did.

The second gospel is that Jesus was in favor of liberation and deliverance from oppression, and you can stand with him in that. This is roughly the gospel of the *theological* Left, and it pretty much turns out to be what the *political* Left also thinks. Is that true? Yes, that is true. A well known preacher of other days, Vance Havner, used to say that Jesus was not crucified for saying, "Behold the lilies; for they toil not, neither do they spin," but for saying, "Behold the Pharisees, how they steal." And from a human point of view, that is what happened. He got under the skin of the oppressors. He was in favor of liberation.

I call the third gospel preached today "churchmanship." Basically, *you take care of your church and your church will take care of you.* Today that is widely practiced in Christianity. Much more widely than people think, and, unfortunately, that "gospel" isn't even true. Now "churchmanship" is important and that is why my wife and I continue to be deeply involved in our local congregation. A lot of people get disillusioned with the church and they don't know quite what to make of it. People sometimes ask me why, since I'm *such* a "profound thinker," I'm still involved in church. I sometimes reply, "Well, the Bible says you're supposed to love your enemies and you'll find a few there." I mean to be humorous, of course, but I sensed some recognition out there as I say that. Actually, however, that is what the church is. It is a place where you can get really mad at people and not run off and leave them. It is a place where anger and contempt can be unlearned. It's a place to learn the deep things of a fellowship in Christ that lovingly endures disagreement, anger, and injury. "Churchmanship" in that sense is important. It is vital. It is in God's plan and nothing is going to take the place of it. The church is intended to be a school of love.

But what we've arrived at in North America is wall-to-wall non-discipleship Christianity. The three gospels that I've mentioned do not produce disciples who naturally move into progressive character transformation. They don't do that, and we all can know it through observation. The three gospels define discipleship in different ways—if they deal with it at all—but always in a way that will not include character transformation and routine obedience. These gospels produce only consumers of religious goods and services, not apprentices to Jesus in kingdom living. We need to ask, if the gospels preached today were the ones originally preached, would there be such a thing as Christianity now? I don't think so. It is now accepted that you can be a Christian forever and not become a disciple. A disciple is someone who is with Jesus learning to be like him. That's a disciple. Actually, that's a disciple in any area. A child in third grade learning long division is a disciple of their teacher. They're with them learning to be like them with respect to a certain discipline. That's what discipleship is. If I'm a disciple of Jesus, I'm learning from him how to lead my life in the kingdom of God as he would lead my life in the kingdom of God if he were in my place. How would he do that? I'm learning from him, I'm not learning to lead his life. He did very well with that and that's done and over with, and we don't need to do that again. What is at issue now is *my* life. How am I going to lead my life?

This brings us back to the issue of the evangelicals in political life. If you're involved in politics, how do you do what you do there—as a judge, a state representative, or chairman of a committee in a political campaign? How would Jesus do that? You must exalt him in your mind to the point where you believe he would actually know how to do the job and do it out the top. So, in so many ways the great old text "What think ye of Christ?" is always the question before us, and if you think of him rightly you will naturally (supernaturally) become his student. You'll become his apprentice and you'll believe that he's the best man in your field, whatever your field is. So this takes him out of the category of merely a sacrificial lamb and puts him in the category of master of the universe. People who are running for the presidency are trying to get a job from

The Failure of Evangelical Political Involvement

Jesus. Did you know that? Jesus is actually now the King of the kings of the earth (Rev 1:5). He's not waiting for the Millennium, though that will change the scene radically. This is now, so the question is how would you be President of the United States and do it like Jesus would do it under present conditions?

We have managed, curiously enough, to get to a place where evangelicals can become "nominal" Christians. This is a real historical curiosity, because one of the things that have been distinctive of evangelicals through the ages—from Luther on—is their resistance to nominal Christianity. But now it is possible for evangelical Christians to differ from non-Christians only or very largely in terms of what they're called. So, when we ask the question we started with—"Why after 25–30 years of evangelical...?"—we have this nominal Christianity as our answer. *The lack of a noteworthy difference in the moral character of public and political life is to be expected from the very nature of contemporary evangelicalism.*

An outstanding church just recently discovered that involvement in church activities is no measure of spiritual growth! I love these people dearly; they're wonderful followers of Christ. But my heart bleeds for them and for us, and I wonder how they could have missed this for so long. Thank God they knew something was not working right, and they went out of their way to make a very elaborate study. But it is the gospel that is preached which establishes the background for evangelical practice, and you cannot "plow around it." You simply can't. That language comes out of frontier days when you deadened trees to plant crops and just "plowed around them" until they fell over. But you can't plow around the central message we are preaching. It determines the result we get. We have to come to grips with that. What are we preaching? What is the message?

The result we get is the natural outcome of the basic message we are preaching, and that outcome is shocking to some people. What is the alternative? Well, we can try preaching the gospel Jesus preached in the way he preached it. We could try that. In my own life as a young, very green Southern Baptist pastor it came as a shock to me when I realized that Jesus was not preaching what I was preaching, and then I realized that I had been taught that I was not supposed to preach what he was preaching. In fact, in one way or another, that teaching has become standard. We today do not know how to preach what he preached. The idea grows up that Paul had one gospel and Jesus had another, which is patently false once you look at the texts. You'd never get that idea from the New Testament unless you were told it *must* be there.

THE DISAPPEARANCE OF MORAL KNOWLEDGE

Around the middle of the last century (after WWII), *knowledge* of good and evil, right and wrong, virtue and vice, ceased to be available from our schools (especially higher education), and then from our churches. We often get the order of events wrong when we start to talk about what has happened in education with the elimination of Bible reading and prayer from public schools. That elimination comes along way down the line. It only happened because of what had happened in higher education decades before. After the WWII, the change in climate of thought began to hit the street level and the court system. But the real issue here was the disappearance of *knowledge* of good and evil, right and wrong, from society. And I emphasize "knowledge" because we're talking about moral knowledge: about *knowing* what is good, what is right, what is wrong and so on. This knowledge ceased to be available *as knowledge* from our schools, but it had much earlier already dropped out of the position of knowledge in elite intellectual circles and in higher education.

Toward the end of the 1800s the university system began to distance itself from the church, as is well known; and one essential way it had of doing that was to interpret theology and morality in such a way that they were no longer counted as knowledge. This process started with some "theology" and with other "ecclesiastical" matters that were taught at the various colleges but were, in fact, just traditions. Usually the particular schools or universities had some denominational identification, and they were each trying to teach *their* "faith and practice" as a whole as if it all amounted to knowledge—though it was largely just tradition. When the emphasis on research came along in higher education, the traditional material often did not stand up to critical examination, and so, rather than sorting it out progressively, to distinguish the sound from the unsound, there simply arose a *redefinition* of what knowledge was. Institutions of "knowledge" ceased to make the traditional moral knowledge—of what kind of persons we ought to be and of what we ought to do—available.[2]

---

2. This process has been carefully studied by Julie Ruben in her *The Making of the Modern University: Intellectual Transformation and the Marginalization of Morality* (Chicago: University of Chicago Press, 1991).

The universities no longer *explicitly* undertook to teach people how to live (although they certainly continued to do so *implicitly*). Gradually there disappeared any responsibility on the part of universities to teach what is right, wrong, good, evil and so on. The background assumption or excuse was that there is no knowledge of such things, so why not do what seems best to you? Some may wonder, for example, how we've arrived (as recently reported in the news) at the point of teaching tantric sex on a certain campus, when something like that couldn't have happened before. Some may think, "Well it's just because we used to be governed by prejudice and now we're open minded." But the things that occur on campus now actually come into a vacuum left by the disappearance of moral knowledge. We have moved from the age of "Why?" seeking a good reason for what we do, to the age of "Why not?" No one in an official position is prepared to go to the people who are doing morally questionable things and even ask, "Why?" I will not begin to tell you stories about what happens in the classroom itself, because in the classroom it's perfectly all right to be *radical* and to relentlessly teach a "radical" morality or religion. You can't be traditional, but you can be radical—that is even a plus to most minds—and then in a pinch you can pass that off as political, not as moral. The political, as we know, does not require knowledge. It only requires advocacy, and that opens the door for things like tantric sex and almost anything else admitting of "consent."

So, in fact, higher education and the elite professional groups continue to pressure and teach on moral matters—good, bad, right, wrong—and if you don't believe it just get crossways of what is advocated in morality by them and you will be subjected to full blown moral opprobrium. That's because in fact no one can separate life from morality. Moral sentiment and moral opinions are always in full force, and perhaps more so now than ever, because *they are not subject to rational criticism in open discussion.* One of the things that used to happen in higher education and elite circles, though certainly not in a perfect way, was that moral teachings were surfaced, talked about, and subjected to rational criticism. Now they're not. What is taught is taught by example, tone of voice, selection of subject matters and so on—oftentimes by unguarded explicit statements—but there's *no rational criticism* directed at them because it's not taken to be an area of rationality or knowledge. Pressure, however, abounds.

Why does it matter whether or not there is moral *knowledge*? This is really the heart of the matter: Knowledge alone confers the right and responsibility to act, to direct action, to set policy, to supervise policy and to teach. Sentiment does not do that. Opinion does not do that. Tradition does not do that. Power does not do that. You expect people who act to *know* what they are doing, don't you? You probably would not take your car to a shop that said on a sign in front of it, "We are *lucky* at making repairs," or "We're inspired," or "We feel real good about it." This is not a matter of convention. It is *how knowledge actually works in human life*, and it's very important to understand that. Without moral knowledge there is no moral authority. Hence there is only "political correctness," even though it looks and feels every bit like morality and often assumes a distinctly moral tone and force.

The upshot is that we fall into calling evil good and good evil. One way of doing that is to say it's all the same—as "diversity" has a way of dictating. In the absence of public knowledge of good and evil, right and wrong, and virtue and vice, *human leaders have no moral basis upon which to lead in terms of what is good*, and so any attempt at leadership in the political, legislative, or other realm immediately becomes a matter of a political or legal contest. There's no acknowledged basis, no public knowledge, of right and wrong, good and evil, in terms of which leadership could be exercised. There's no basis upon which to guide a leader's personal life and public choices, and as a result leaders tend to abdicate to public or internal pressures with no basis to support them in goodness. Desire, pleasure, and success guide them. Personal integrity rarely survives, still less does effectiveness in leading for what is good and right.

Today, equality is not actually regarded as a matter of human dignity and value. That is very hard to defend. Rather it is regarded as a doorway to freedom. Freedom itself is not regarded in terms of the inherent dignity and value of human beings, but rather as *opportunity*. Opportunity is not regarded as opportunity to do what is good and right, but *to get what you want*. We talk a lot about them, but the basic values in our society are not equality and freedom—they are pleasure and happiness. And these are interpreted in sensualistic terms. Our society is a society of *feeling*. That is why debt conquers common sense. Feeling is our master. That's why we have so many issues about abuse of one kind or another—abuse comes out of frustration over feeling. That is why we are such an addictive society. Also, watch your commercials for automobiles, etc., and see how much of it is predicated upon feeling. Feeling runs our society. It also runs our massively failing educational system. It is the only acknowledged ultimate value. That explains why we do so badly in areas of learning that require sustained discipline—it doesn't feel good. Our society basically has two values, which come together. One is doing what you want to do—mistaken for freedom—and the other is pleasure. Sometimes people say happiness is one of our values, but happiness now means nothing that would have been recognized as such by the great thinkers from Aristotle to John Locke, for it translates simply into pleasure—having a good time. (That is how tantric sex becomes interesting to Lutherans and Baptists, etc. Much of what Bill Clinton learned about sex—what is and is not "sex with that woman"—he learned in legalistic religion.) The disappearance of *knowledge* of moral values leaves us open to all sorts of delusions.

On the subject of freedom, I want to recommend a work by a man named Thomas Hill Green, called *Lectures on the Principles of Political Obligation*.[3] What you find in Green is the efforts of a man who was raised an evangelical and grew more liberal as he went on in his life, but he retained a sense of what freedom *should* mean. He argued that freedom is not just freedom *from*; freedom is the exercise of abilities to attain the good in community. This bears repeating: *Freedom is the exercise of abilities to attain the good in community.* If you want to see real freedom made visible, watch Pavarotti in performance. That's freedom. Watch a highly disciplined athlete, *sans* drugs. You'll see freedom. If you follow the idea of freedom in Thomas Hill Green's writings, you will understand that this connection between freedom and good *is* an area of knowledge. We must learn to represent it as such.

PROFESSIONAL CALLING FAILS

In the past, human beings had access to the support of a religious outlook like the one that characterized *classical* evangelicalism, in people like Richard Baxter and John Wesley or William Wilberforce. When we think of Wilberforce, it's important to remember that there were two objectives on his part. One was the abolition of the slave trade. For this he is admired today and got a movie made about him. But there was also the "reformation of manners," as he called it. It is important to look at his book[4] that

---

3. Thomas Hill Green, *Lectures on the Principles of Political Obligation* (New York: Longmans, Green, 1895).

4. Wilberforce, William, *A Practical View of the Prevailing Religious System of Professed Christians, in the Higher and Middle Classes in This Country, Contrasted with Real Christianity* (London: Cadell and Davies, 1797). There are many editions, but try to

was written to address the issue of "manners" and ask yourself how many evangelicals of today would be comfortable with what it says. It's written out of a specific theological context. John Wesley and John Newton shared and promoted its outlook, and it presents a very different perspective on real Christianity from anything we would recognize as evangelical today—no matter how heartily we sing "Amazing Grace."

With the absence of publically available knowledge of the good and the right, and of any essential relationship with the Christian gospel, the traditional understanding of *professional* devotion to the good in one's profession serves is lost. When knowledge of good and devotion to God ceases to be the governing principle of professional life, then professional integrity collapses or shrinks down to mere technical competence. Now, in the theory of the professions as it's being done today, you see the gradual but inevitable disappearance of any idea of devotion to the public good. It's very interesting to see how market theory enters the picture. The only obligation of the professional, it is increasingly said, is technical expertise, and in the context in which individuals use and exercise that expertise the market will—we vainly imagine—sort out who's good and who's bad, and competition will make things all work for the best for the public. Yes, and about then another cow flew by.

The Rotary slogan, by contrast, is "Service above self"—which is still displayed at the meetings. You don't have to wonder where that came from, right? That's Jesus, and people knew that and honored that when they started the Rotary Club. They knew that and thus they had a *moral vision of professional life*, which remained very strong in this country up until quite recently—again, finally caving in to the influence of the academy. But what could the slogan mean today? With the demise of Christian moral understanding as a bulwark of public life, it certainly does not have the power to oblige. Really, it means hardly anything at all. Still, "Service above self" is the idea in back of traditional professionalism, and if you have a Christian vision of life in the kingdom of God as a disciple of Jesus—and on the basis of that you have moral knowledge and a corresponding moral life—then you're prepared to become a very different kind of person in public service. You will not live for your self-advance-

---

find an unabridged version. Read it along with William Law, *A Serious Call to a Devout and Holy Life, Adapted to the State and Condition of All Orders of Christians* (London: J. Richardson, [172-]).

ment above all, but seek to advance the causes of what is good and right in your special field of activity—the political above all.

IS THERE A WAY BACK?

You will not be surprised to hear me say that there is. There is a way back, but it is the way of Jesus Christ, understood now in the generous but rigorous way that it has been understood for much of the past in this country, and in other countries in other parts of the world. There is a way back, but evangelical leaders (pastors, teachers, writers) must lead. *They are the ones who have to lead the way back.* They will find many others to join them if they will but lead. One of the things that will happen for those who follow Christ fully and grow in their relationship to him is that they will stand out in such a way that people will look to them for leadership. There's a very interesting incident in the history of the Huguenots. For many centuries there's been an ongoing battle between Islam and the rest of the world. It is not a new thing. There was a period in which those under Islam ran sea galleys around the Mediterranean—ships run by oars, and those oars pulled by slaves. It's interesting that on those galleys the Huguenots were the ones that everyone trusted. If they had anything of value to be kept, they put it in the care of the Huguenot. If there was any issue of truth or righteousness, the Huguenots on board were the ones who were looked to for right judgment. That is an example of what we were looking at in Philippians 2 above, of shining out as lights in a darkened world.

Our point of attack and of service today must be the presentation of the basic biblical truths as knowledge of reality. What the world has done is to negotiate the church into a position of saying that it does not have knowledge. Christians just have faith, and faith is an irrational leap. The world assumes Archie Bunker's definition of faith: "It's what you wouldn't believe for your life if it wasn't in the Bible." This is a total misunderstanding of faith. Although faith often goes beyond knowledge, it *never* works—on the biblical model—outside of a context of knowledge. Many of the things we as Christians have faith in are things we also actually know—or can know. That will seem almost cognitively incoherent for most people today, because they've had it ground into them that when it comes to faith, knowledge is simply ruled out. That's why it is hard to make any sense of "separation of church and state" *as it is discussed today*, in comparison to how it was understood in the writing of the Constitution, which makes perfect sense. People today think of something other than knowledge when you say "church." If the church brought vital knowledge to human existence, there would be no more talk of separation of church and state, *in its current meaning*, than there would be separation of chemistry and state. In the past it was assumed that the church *did* bring vital knowledge to human existence.

It was basically the decision of the church itself to let knowledge go, in the 1800s and 1900s, and to undertake to present something other than vital *knowledge*. That decision set the scene for where we stand now. I'm talking about knowledge as you require it in your dentist, your auto mechanic, your brain surgeon, your politician (I hope) and so on. You have knowledge of a subject matter when you are representing it (speaking of it, treating it) *as it is*, on an *appropriate basis* of thought and experience—including a proper use of "authority." Most of the things we know, scientific or otherwise, we know on the basis of authority. Somebody told us. There is nothing wrong with that. What is presented in the Bible on fair interpretation, and verifiable in life, is knowledge of reality—especially of the spiritual and moral life in Christ. So if you're going to turn things back to genuine character transformation, you have to resist the temptation to shy away from presenting the basic things—let's call it "mere Christianity," it's a good phrase—as knowledge. You have to shy away from treating these things as something else, such as feelings, opinions, traditions, power plays. You have to know and accept and present mere Christianity as a *body of knowledge*.

What do I mean? To repeat: *You have knowledge of a subject matter where you are representing it as it is, on an appropriate basis of thought and experience*. So, let's try the Apostles' Creed: "I believe in God, the Father almighty, creator of heaven and earth. I believe in Jesus Christ, God's only Son, our Lord," and so forth. Is that knowledge? What do you say? The challenge is to stand up for Christian *knowledge*. Not with dogmatism or close-mindedness, but with all humility of mind, with all openness, ready to hear anything from anyone. But you must represent it as knowledge if you are going to find the way back to an evangelicalism that is routinely transformational. The disastrous mistake was that the church backed away from knowledge in the last two centuries, and piously proclaimed "faith" as something superior to and indifferent to knowledge. But the Bible is all about knowledge. Just read the texts with that in mind. Do inductive bible study on "knowledge." Even eternal life is knowledge, as Jesus said (John

17:3), and as we see in 2 Peter 1:2–5, where we are told that we've been provided with "everything pertaining to life and godliness, through the true knowledge of Him who called us by His own glory and excellence." It's all founded upon knowledge, though there is more to discipleship to Christ than just knowledge.

Vital knowledge is of course never what we now call "head knowledge," and that's the way the Bible treats it. It is *interactive relationship*. When Jesus says, "This is eternal life, that they may know You, the only true God, and Jesus Christ whom You have sent" (John 17:3), he's talking about *interactive relationship*. That's knowledge—biblical knowledge. Now of course "head knowledge" can come out of that, but life knowledge is always interactive relationship.

There is also the idea of "secular knowledge" that must be confronted. Allowing the secular world to *define* knowledge means there would be no knowledge of God, and the Christian would be left with mere scraps of "tradition" and "diversity." But what business does a university have being secular? Think about it for a moment: *secular* university? Is reality secular? George Bernard Shaw used to say that "Catholic University" is an oxymoron. What he had in mind, that clever but shallow man, was that if you were Catholic you had to be close-minded. Well, maybe he needed to broaden his acquaintance with Catholics. There certainly are close-minded ones, as with people of every group, including the secular. But if "Catholic University" is an oxymoron, then why isn't "secular university"? I submit to you that it is just that, and if you ever want to see close-mindedness and thoughtlessness, step into the atmosphere of a secular university. Is reality secular? Has someone shown that it's secular? No. There isn't even a division of the university that's called the "Reality Department." They don't even have one. It's a little presumptuous for a university to pronounce itself secular, isn't it?

Having lost knowledge, people today are no longer in a position to deal seriously with moral issues. The basic content of moral knowledge is actually love. Love is so central that you cannot ignore it, and everyone knows that it is *somehow* the mark of a good person. We want to be tough intellectually so we don't want to use that word very much in "serious" academic contexts. Thus, twentieth-century ethical theory can be accurately characterized as an effort to have morality without a heart. We've surely seen how *that* works. Remember that John Dewey argued we should want to be good, but not "goody-goody."[5] So everyone is busy not being "goody," and good disappears as a factor governing rational life.

The good person is one permeated with *agape* love. Right action is the action of love. To love is to be devoted to the good of what is loved. I love those around me as I am working for their good, and of course mine too, under God; and Jesus and his followers deal with the details of this at great lengths. No one has ever come close to spelling out what love means as he did. We have a terrible time understanding love because we confuse it with desire. We say things like, "I love chocolate cake." Now, for sure you do not love chocolate cake. You want to eat it. That's different. I suppose you could imagine someone who actually loved chocolate cake. They'd just go around taking care of chocolate cakes, watching out for their interests. We have an awfully hard time today making sense of love because we're so confused on these matters. But once we pay attention, we realize that desire is not love, and often is *opposed* to love. In this country, every fifteen seconds (I think it is) some woman is badly beaten—maybe killed—by someone, usually one who says he "loves" her.

The path to moral goodness comes through Jesus Christ. The path toward becoming a thoroughly good person, dominated by love, is apprenticeship to Jesus Christ in the kingdom of God. A disciple of Jesus is one learning from him to live his/her life in the way Jesus would live it. And now we're back to the issue of who has the responsibility for bringing this out: it is the pastors and the teachers—primarily of the evangelical churches. Most of the other churches have fallen completely under the sway of the university system with its moral blindness. The good news in the gospel of the New Testament is that we can now enter the rule and reign of God by relying upon Jesus for everything. We do that by becoming like little children, as Jesus said, by going "beyond the righteousness of the scribes and Pharisees" (beyond performance into the depths of the heart), and by being born "from above." Those are words chosen from Jesus' teachings about entering the Kingdom of the Heavens or the kingdom of God.

Salvation then becomes not about the afterlife, but about the life that comes into us *now*—enters us by the Spirit of God from above. Above is right here. It is resurrection life. That is salvation. Paul says in 1 Corinthians 15:17, "If Christ has not been raised, your faith is worthless; you are still in

---

5. John Dewey, *Democracy and Education* (New York: McMillan, 1916), 414.

your sins." *Redemption does not stop at the cross*, it moves on from there. In 2 Corinthians 5:14–15 we read, "One died for all, therefore all died; and He died for all, so that . . ."—and how would you finish that sentence? I'm disappointed in you! You got it right: ". . . so that they who live might no longer live for themselves, but for Him who died and rose again on their behalf." You were supposed to say, as good evangelicals, ". . . so that people can be forgiven and go to heaven." Do you see the difference? If you have a theory of the atonement that does not take in life now, you don't have it right about the atonement Christ provides. Moral maturity and integrity come through growth in the grace and knowledge of our Lord and Savior Jesus Christ. (2 Peter 3:18) Grace itself is *God interacting in our lives*. It's interactive relationship, the very place of knowledge of God. You grow in the grace and the knowledge of our Lord Jesus Christ as your life is increasingly dominated by interactive relationship to Christ in everything. That's what it means to grow in spiritual and moral maturity. The things that Jesus teaches in the Sermon on the Mount simply illustrate the life of the person living and growing in the kingdom of God. They show that the life that comes out as we study under him is routine, easy obedience. We shift out of where people are now, standing in ordinary fallen relationships, where they might, for example, wonder why you would want to tell the truth if it might cost you something. Instead you honestly come to think and say, "Why would I want to tell a lie? Why? Why would I want to mislead someone since I'm standing in the kingdom of God, since God is with me and I'm growing in his kind of life?" "Do not lie to one another, *since you laid aside the old self with its evil practices*" (Col 3:9; emphasis added).

Spiritual disciplines—necessary components of life with Christ—are simply activities that we undertake, activities in our power. They are something *we do* that enables us to disrupt evil habits and patterns in our lives and *receive* grace to enable us to grow increasingly toward easy, routine obedience to Christ. They are not laws. They are not righteousness. They are simply wisdom. They are age-old and life-tested, and we need to use them in our relationship with Christ. The grace of God will then flow more richly into our lives. Solitude, silence, fasting, worship, fellowship—all those are disciplines that help us receive more of divine life in our human circumstances.

Now, my final hammer blow here is that evangelical pastors and teachers are in a position to bring to their people and to the public a knowledge that will guide life into the goodness and blessedness of the Kingdom of the Heavens. That was Christ's intention in giving us his "Great Commission." He said in kingdom proclamation, "I have been given say over all things in heaven and earth. As you go make disciples, surround them in Trinitarian reality . . ." That's what you do with disciples. You don't just get them wet while you say, "In the name of the Father, Son, and Holy Spirit" over them. Jesus said, "Where two or three have gathered together in My name, I am there in their midst." (Matt 18:20) We use that passage when only two or three show up. But actually it's true in the case where two or three *thousand* are gathered in his name—if they truly gather in his name and he's the one running the show.

They're then in a position to teach disciples to do *everything that Jesus said*. That's the natural progression. Then—as in past times—you will see emerging a people stunningly different from those who are children of darkness and who walk in the kingdom of darkness. The pastors are to be the teachers of the nations. The Christian writers and teachers are to teach the nations. That's their call. They teach their knowledge—their knowledge of God, their knowledge of the human soul. They have to stand in the dignity of *that* calling and insist upon it, not out of arrogance but out of humility, and out of the firm realization that they must bring to human beings something that is both absolutely essential and something that no one else can bring.

Christian schools (Christian "higher education") have to stand *with* pastors in that posture. Perhaps the greatest issue facing the church today is whether or not Christian schools will say loudly and clearly that they have *essential knowledge* that non-Christian schools do not have. There is a great resistance to this among Christian educators. The old line—sometimes called "mainline"—churches were betrayed by their schools. A great issue facing us today is whether or not the evangelical church will be betrayed by its schools. The great issue is whether or not the evangelical schools will say, "We have knowledge—knowledge that the world and the so-called secular universities do not have. We have knowledge. We're not just 'nicer' and rather odd."

The ancient writers such as Plato and Aristotle believed that the administration of law and political life was the highest of merely human callings. The highest, because in it the greatest of human good and evil was at issue. But humanity should know by now, given its track record,

The Failure of Evangelical Political Involvement

that it is a calling that can only be carried out in a wisdom and power that is beyond the human. The evangelical message and life in its classical forms—not that of post-WWII evangelicalism—shows how that can be done. There is no real alternative in human existence. It isn't because evangelicals are superior in any other respect. And it isn't that people we call "evangelicals" are the only brand of Christians who must and can do such public service. It is simply the call of Christ to his followers, who say now as long ago, "'Lord, to whom shall we go? You have the words of eternal life'" (John 6:68).

7

Practical Ways Forward

Donald McConnell

CHRISTIANS TODAY ARE RETHINKING our approach to politics, law, evangelism, missions, and life. In the political and legal realms, despite some success and progress, we have faced what is perceived as betrayal, failure, and decay. While prayer clubs are now allowed on many campuses, our religious liberties seem to be forever under siege. Though we have won the right for states to restrict abortions in some ways, abortion on demand is still legal nearly everywhere and new technologies threaten to multiply the mass killing of tiny humans—many to be created for liquidation to exploit their organs and tissues. Honesty and character seem to be in short supply among the governing classes, and we have been betrayed and let down by those who claimed to be our friends. Other areas of public policy seem torn between unacceptable extremes: If we let the world have its way, it will criminalize fidelity to certain moral truths, and if we resist, it will still teach our children that we are bigots of the worst kind because we cling to what the Bible and every advanced moral teaching of the ages has taught. As in all times, the evils of our time are a sufficient challenge for our day.

Many are discouraged by the evils of our day. But we need not be. God is still sovereign. He still answers prayer. History shows that our day is not the worst or the most threatening of all days yet. And there is much we can do. We still have a great deal of freedom to do what we can do. I have nine recommendations for dealing with these times and seeking a reformation of our approach to human law and government.

Practical Ways Forward

UNDERSTAND OUR FALLIBILITY, BUT OVERCOME IT

First, we need to recognize our human fallibility, but we should not be stopped by that. As Christians we recognize that we are all sinful human beings and that all human beings are fallen, so we have to be humble. It is true that we will get things wrong. It is true that we will make mistakes. It is true that we will not ever have perfect candidates to run for office. And it is also true that, no matter how hard we try, we will not always have what we would consider success; but God doesn't call us to not take risks. God calls us to a life of moral adventure.

Think of the parable of the talents: the master gave so many talents to one servant, and so many to another, and so many to another. Two servants invested well and God rewarded them, but one of the servants took his talent and buried it in the ground to hide it. When the master returned, he was displeased that the servant played it safe with his money instead of investing it in some profitable enterprise. We often use this parable as a sermon illustration to talk about using the gifts God has given us. In fact, that's how the word "talent," which used to mean an amount of money, came to mean the gifts or abilities God has given you. But it really means something else as well. It means that God wants us to be willing to take reasonable risks in life. The Christian life is not meant to be played safe. It is meant to be a moral adventure in which we go out and make tough choices and tough calls and tough decisions. We take a risk when we share the gospel with a neighbor. We have to take a risk to plant a church. We have to take a risk to preach the gospel in a place where it is illegal to do so. And, we have to take risks to bring about a better legal or political regime, order, or status. We have to take risks in order to really live the life that Christ has called us to live to the hilt. There's risk involved in our judgment about what the best course of action is, even after prayerful consideration. One course may be wrong, but it is better to take that risk and occasionally be wrong than to bury our talent in the earth and not take any chances. God will help us if we obey what he's asked us to do; if we obey his commandments. So the risk of failure is not an excuse for staying out of the political game, or for failing to help see to it that our neighbors have good laws. God uses earthen vessels like us to do his will. We need to be willing to be used.

ALL OF HUMANITY IS FALLEN

Second, we need to recognize the fallenness of humankind, not only of ourselves. This is one of those things that is profoundly different between the law from a few centuries ago and that of today. People were very aware of human fallibility during the age in which the common law first developed. People knew God's moral law required perfection but that human beings were quite incapable of achieving perfection. This fact means human law has to have an inherent compromise in it. All human laws are compromises, because government cannot require perfection. If we did, keeping in mind that "the wages of sin is death" (Rom 6:23) and that "all have sinned and fall short of the glory of God" (Rom 3:23), we'd have to execute all of us if we were going to apply God's moral law as the law of the state. We obviously can't do that. So there will always be a difference between the civic law of the state and the moral law of God.

Even if you look at ancient Israel, God made compromises with them in matters of civil law. In Matthew 19, Jesus points out that God allowed the Israelites to have divorces even though that wasn't in the heart of God. If you've ever looked at the city of refuge system in the Old Testament as well, it's a wonderful metaphor about salvation, but it's also an interesting compromise. I don't think God really wanted avengers of blood to go out and kill people who had committed negligent homicide. But God recognized that in the culture of that day, there would be people who would not be willing to give up the idea of the blood feud in which relatives avenge the deaths of their relations. So God created a system to try to mitigate that evil cultural artifact. He didn't just ignore it. So even in the Old Testament God made accommodation for human inability to perfectly keep the moral law. Modern human laws must do that as well. Practical human laws are never going to require people to do everything they should do, or prevent people from doing everything they shouldn't. And, indeed, laws alone cannot achieve much.

The Reformers believed that law could achieve what they called "civic righteousness." Good civic laws could keep people from murdering each other and robbing each other wholesale. Proper legal deterrents could keep people living as reasonably good neighbors. But the Reformers also said the law cannot make men and women moral. It cannot turn them into people who have the right feelings. It cannot make them into people who take the right, affirmative steps toward each other. It cannot turn them into people who give to each other all that we owe each other under the debt of love.

By the same token, human laws have to fit in with moral law. They shouldn't contradict it. The state shouldn't require people to do things that God forbids, or forbid people to do things that God requires. But we cannot think that through human law we can make up for the fall, or that we can perfect humans. Certainly, the last century is a terrible example. Think of all the different regimes that thought that if they only controlled education, if they only controlled raising children, if they only controlled all of the workplaces, if they only had all the strings and all the reins, they could force people to become the "new Soviet man." They could make them perfect, altruistic people that always gave and never took. These regimes were perfectly willing to murder huge numbers of people and torture other people in order to try to force everyone else to be perfect, but it still did not work. So, we have to be careful about utopian schemes—people like to think we can do away with all of the effects of the fall through law, through government, through human education, but we cannot.

In the same vein, Jesus had some similar advice for lawyers on the topic of making and enforcing rules and laws. In Luke 11, we read that Jesus said that the lawyers in the Sanhedrin were guilty of placing burdens on people that no one could carry, and not lifting one finger to help others with those burdens. We need to be careful as evangelicals involved with helping our neighbors in the political realm not to lay unbearable burdens—burdens we cannot bear, burdens others cannot bear.

COMMITMENT TO THE TRUTH

Third, we need to have commitment to truth. We've talked about this a great deal in this book already. What Dallas Willard argued about belief in real knowledge was very significant. The knowledge that we have of God and his moral truths, and of the universal ideals such as justice, beauty, truth, and goodness—which flow from who God is and what he is like—are critical for law and government. These are things we have let slip from our grasp, and yet they are so fundamental to everything. When the synthesis of the Western legal system occurred in the Middle Ages, nearly everyone at the time believed in the reality of moral knowledge—they knew about God, they knew about good and evil, they knew about justice and truth and beauty and the good—and this knowledge was a key to what a good state, a good city, a good government was like, and how it was run. Nothing could be allowed to contradict the good. They knew they couldn't make people perfect, but they didn't try to make them evil either. They knew they should not pass laws that required evil things. They knew laws should not limit the freedom to choose among natural goods and pursue them. If, by contrast, we do not know the difference between good and evil, or justice and injustice, if all we have is interests and values and desires, then we're in big trouble because we can't run a just legal system that way. Yet today, most of our universities and many of our pulpits teach people the latter and not the former. We deny knowledge of the building blocks necessary for a good civil society and teach people to be skeptical in ways that are corrosive to a civil society. Our society has become like the scribes and Pharisees who Jesus said, in Luke 11:52, had hidden the key to knowledge, neither using it themselves nor letting others. If we are to reform law and government, we must restore the wisdom and knowledge that comes from God to a central place in our hearts, minds, plans, and policies.

We've tried to live with less and less truth in many ways in America. We've tried to run a legal system based on all of us saying, "Oh, I want this!" "I want that!" "Don't stop me from doing this!" and then basically competing with each other to see how much we can grab if we get together in groups and brawl about who's going to get what. That's no way to run a country and no way to make laws. Somehow, we have to convince people again that the good, the true, the beautiful, and the just are genuinely knowable and discoverable, and that God has put these things in our hearts and minds. We must convince them that these are right within our grasp if we will but seek them, and seek him, because God himself is the embodiment of all truth. He is the truth, so the knowledge of God, the knowledge of Christ, and the knowledge of the good, the true, the beautiful, and all these things are tied together. They are a unity. Somehow we need to remember they are united and refute the postmodernism that says that there are no truths, only different stories.

We need to reject the classic skepticism of the Enlightenment that really destroyed the belief in moral knowledge. We need to reject the idea of radical, political liberalism: that the truths about God and the good and justice have no place in politics, no place in law and no place in government. We need to reject the extreme individualism in our society that wants to make every person his or her own god. We need to not fall prey to the radical communitarianism out there waiting in the wings which says, "Well, let's just make the community god, then." Instead, we need to pay attention to who the real God is and to let his truths rule over us.

Even Plato, who was no Christian, knew that a community should not have humans rule over them because they're too arrogant. They're too conceited. They seek their own interests. Instead, we have to have law rule over us. That spark of the divine is how they thought of it, and we know a little better. We know about the divine logos that gives light to every man. So we have to recover that as knowledge—as a basis for society. Dallas Willard talked a little about separation of church and state. Separation of church and state was meant to separate the hierarchy of organized churches from the hierarchy of the state. It was not meant to separate the truth about reality from the minds of those who make laws or who govern. There are things you can't just ignore, such as science. The government can't just say, "We don't believe in electricity. We're going to pretend it doesn't exist. We are going to govern without electricity." No, we have to pay attention to reality. And God is also real. Morality is real. The good, the true, and the beautiful are real, and so we can't govern without paying attention to those things. We can't pretend that it isn't there, any more than we can pretend that fire, or cold, or electricity isn't there. This is something that we have to convince people about once again because our society has completely lost that knowledge and that vision. We have been guilty, in a sense, of letting society lose it by falling prey to all sorts of philosophies about life and knowledge that weren't really biblical—that weren't the system that is assumed in the Bible and proclaimed in the Bible.

Now this may be difficult for us because the spirit of our age safeguards itself by proclaiming to people that it is arrogant, mean, bigoted, and unloving to believe in truth or to reject error. We must be careful not to confuse what is clear and unclear, or what is moral and what is indifferent, or the functions of the church and the functions of government. But when a truth is clear, or when an idea is clearly in error, we can be polite and kind in how we proclaim the truth, but we must not deny the truth. Refusing to believe God and act on what he says clearly is the very essence of arrogance, bigotry, and pride, and is a failure to love.

God and Governing

AFFIRM IMPORTANT DISTINCTIONS

We do need to recognize the difference between different kinds of issues. There are some clear moral issues in life: Don't murder people. Don't steal their possessions. Don't encourage people to commit adultery. But most things that politicians and governments deal with are not actually that easy. While the motivation for most laws is moral—protecting innocent human life is behind most traffic laws for example—the choice of which policy will best vindicate and serve the moral principle is often not a choice based on morality. Should fines for speeding be $50 or $100 for example? Some laws involve choosing which risk you prefer. Other government choices involve resolving the pull of competing moral truths and trying to decide which one is more important than the other. Sometimes politics involves choosing which painful, unpleasant thing you prefer more than others. So, sometimes we have to recognize that there are going to be rational differences of opinion about various issues.

We have to get used to the fact that, even among Christians, we will occasionally disagree about things—about whether or not a particular war is a good idea, about whether or not a particular program is a good idea, about whether or not we prefer long or short statutes of limitations, about whether we think we should have tariffs on wool imports or not—and it's perfectly okay to disagree on such issues.

C. S. Lewis was asked if Christian Britons should start a Christian party in the United Kingdom back in the 1930s, as England already had many of the same problems we have now in America. Lewis said no, because he was concerned that if we tried to have a party that was the "Christian party," then its positions on all of the indifferent issues would be thought of by somebody as the "Christian" ones.[1] People would associate, for instance, its position on tariffs on shoes imported from Italy with Christianity, and then people who like Italian shoes would assume that Christians must be mean, nasty people. "They're raising the price of Italian shoes!"

We have to be careful, because some of what politics is about has nothing to do with direct moral principles, and there's certainly room to

---

1. C. S. Lewis, "Meditations on the Third Commandment," in God in the Dock: Essays in Theology and Ethics, edited by Walter Hooper (Grand Rapids: Eerdmans, 1970), 196–99.

disagree. But that's where being kind to other people and having good manners—playing well with others—comes into this. We really need to realize that, not only may we be wrong, but it's perfectly legitimate for our opponent to have a different opinion about things. And if we realize that, we are going to debate things in a different way than if we're on a crusade against immoral infidels. So, it's important to have good manners in politics, to have good character, to be honest with people, to be consistent and not just take the easy way out—in part because politics is full of debatable issues in which we have moral goals, but which different policies may seek to fulfill such goals in different ways and still not be immoral, even though they are different.

REJECT MADISON AVENUE

We also need to reject Madison Avenue. At one time, everything having to do with modern advertising techniques was associated with Madison Avenue, New York, where the big advertising houses were located back in the twenties and thirties. Behind the Madison Avenue mindset is the notion that all challenges can be conquered through the ruthless use of management techniques, manipulative advertising, psychology, polling, and branding. For example, the way companies use attractive women in commercials to tell you what you "desperately need." The advertisement siren purrs: "Are you losing your hair? Try Gro-tex! The hair-restoring potion." And millions respond by running out to buy Gro-tex. It is easy to fall into trying to study and then manipulate people, but it is not the best way to deal with the problems of government, education, or other kinds of activities that are not primarily concerned with selling things. In fact, sometimes it is not even a very good or honest way to sell things. We should not fall into the trap of using the manipulative techniques of the worldly to achieve our political or legal goals.

It's also true that often focus groups and ad gurus give pretty rotten advice, because they are not looking at what is true, good, and beautiful, and telling you to do that. They are looking at a few people they have picked, rather unscientifically, who tell them what they think they want, based on the input already given them. If you are highly skilled, it is possible to get a poll or a focus group to tell you anything you want. They certainly are not going to necessarily tell you the right thing to do. So, while it is important to listen to what people think and pay attention to where people are at, it's a lot more important to lead them in the right direction. People don't always know what they ought to do and what they ought to think unless we explain it to them.

GOD-CENTERED LIVING

We also need to be careful to recognize the connection between who God is and how we should live. This is related to what I was saying before about truth. As Christians, we sometimes tend to look at God as if he were more like the Muslim idea of God—this capricious deity who does whatever he wants and gives us a bunch of rules, and we're just supposed to go out and follow the rules. But the God that we serve is not like that. Ours is the God of Abraham, Isaac, and Jacob; the God who became incarnate among us as Jesus Christ who died for our sins and rose from the dead. His very nature is what is good and true and beautiful. In fact, the definition of the good, the true, and the beautiful is in God himself—it's defined by God himself, by who he is. Everything finds its definition in relation to God. It's either like him or not like him. I think again Plato was on the right track—even for a pagan—when he said, "God is preeminently the measure of all things." If a pagan Greek could figure that out, how much more should we be able to see that when we have the Bible easily available to us.

We need to get to know Christ through the Scriptures. The better we know Jesus, the better we know God the Father, the more we are touched by him, the more we will be transformed and become the people he really wants us to be. If we're going to put on Christ, if we're going to be like him, we need to know who he is and what he's like. That's one of the things I really love about C. S. Lewis. His theology was not always absolutely perfect, but it is very apparent when you read the Chronicles of Narnia, for example, that he really understood who God is and what God is really like. Lewis was able to communicate what God is like in a way that made it accessible to people. As God gave Elisha a double portion of the spirit that he had given Elijah, we need a double portion of the Spirit, as God gave it to C. S. Lewis, so we can see clearly who God is and explain it eloquently to others in discipleship, teaching, preaching, art, literature, and in our lives.

Practical Ways Forward

STAND FOR REAL FREEDOM WITH THE RULE OF LAW

We need to also stand for freedom with the rule of law. Now let me first define "freedom" in the context I am speaking about here. The word has come to mean many things. For purposes of this address, "freedom" is the ability to choose among true goods. I do not disagree with Professor Kennedy's understanding of freedom as belonging, but I am addressing a slightly different concept here. This is a very different definition from the popular conception of freedom today, which is more or less the ability to be your own law or to be your own god. Radical personal autonomy is not real freedom. Because Christians have seen an increased demand for legalization of licentiousness, we sometimes make the mistake of setting ourselves against freedom itself with the thought that human law should be strong and invasive so as to limit public sin. There are public sins like obscenity that can and should be limited by law. But it is a mistake to advocate for the power of government to be increased and true freedom decreased. If we succeeded in this, we would likely find that the power of government to limit speech, control zoning, direct the content of education, supersede parental authority, and limit the activities of businesses and corporations would ultimately come to be used, not by reasonable folk to further civil morality, but by our spiritual enemies to choke off every opportunity to share the gospel or disseminate the truth.

It's always tempting to think that if we could just take over and make everybody do what we want, then everything would be okay. But one of the risks we have to take, one of the necessary moral adventures, is letting people be free to do some of the things they're going to do or not do. Certainly there are areas in which freedom has to be restrained. We can't let people run around murdering others by simply claiming they're not people. It's easy to classify certain groups of people, claim they're not people, and then treat them maliciously. We did that to slaves, we're doing it to the unborn, and there is a growing threat to the aged and infirm. We've done enough of that in the past; we shouldn't do it anymore. But there are some areas where we have to let people be free. If they use their freedom to make wrong choices, then we've got a problem. But people will choose what they will and we can't make them choose Christ. We have to let them be free to be led to Christ or not.

We also need the rule of law. The rule of law is based on the idea that because humans are untrustworthy, we will not entrust all government power to humans; instead we will put the real power in laws that flow from the higher law—the objective moral law of God. Those laws, then, will be binding on everyone, without exception, from pope to pauper and emperor to embryo. This is an old idea and has been foundational to Western civilization. It is implied throughout the Bible and articulated by even pagan writers like Plato and Cicero. We live in a society that is forgetting, or has forgotten, what the rule of law is. In fact there is an amazing essay in Boston University Law Review by a professor I had at the USC School of Law, Margaret Jane Radin, in which she says, in effect: We don't actually believe in the rule of law anymore because we don't believe that there are any objective rules out there; but people like the phrase, so we need to come up with another definition so we can keep using it, yet without meaning what people used to mean by it.[2] Contrary to Professor Radin's apparent view, it is important that we keep not only the term "rule of law" but also its traditional meaning. God is the real sovereign and true law is his regent. Human laws have to reflect and be in line with the moral law, even though human laws have to be compromises from the moral law because none of us can keep the whole of the moral law. If human laws are properly constructed and applied with justice and mercy, they cannot save people or even make people good, but they can, in a relatively Christian society, encourage a sort of civil righteousness in which most people are reasonably good neighbors. The most important aspect of the rule of law is that it makes the imposition of tyranny difficult. To allude to the film *A Man for All Seasons*, if our country is thickly forested with true laws that recognize real rights, restrain evil, promote the common good, provide for justice, allow mercy, and provide for a real due process that is about truth and dignity, we will have a shelter and a hiding place from the naked use of political power.

We need the rule of law. But we also need a lot of freedom—freedom of religion, freedom of speech, freedom of assembly. We Christians are going to be the first people to lose our freedom if we ever decide to take away other people's freedoms. The minute we start saying we're not going to let the adherents of a religion or an idea talk to people, those laws will be used against us and we'll be the people who can't talk to anybody.

2. Margaret Jane Radin, "Reconsidering the Rule of Law," Boston University Law Review 69 (1989) 781–814; also reprinted in edited form in Robert L Hayman Jr. et al, editors, Jurisprudence, Classical and Contemporary: From Natural Law to Positivism, 2nd ed. (St. Paul: West Group, 2002) 775–81.

Freedom without law and morality becomes mere license. Law without freedom is grim indeed. To be faithful participants in the political process, we must hang onto both freedom and the rule of law.

ENCOURAGE THE VOCATIONS OF LAW AND POLITICS

This point is related to the old country-western song, "Mamas, Don't Let Your Babies Grow Up To Be Cowboys." Well, I'd like to say to parents: please let your children grow up to be lawyers and statesmen. We in the evangelical world are happy when our children grow up to become pastors, teachers, or missionaries, but I think a lot of parents become a bit nervous if little Jane or Johnny is interested in law school. They probably should be, because, as I'll describe in a minute, law school can be a little dangerous.

We have to have people who are statesmen and who are lawyers, and who do those jobs well. Not just in the presidency, but also in the school board and all that is in between. If we do not raise our young people to have civic responsibility, then we will continue to have more of the same problems we have now. We actually need the people among us who are exhibiting the best character to become political leaders, instead of just the people who are the best at remembering names and kissing babies. It should be seen as a duty.

CLASSICAL EDUCATION

To put young people in mind of such duties, and to equip them to do what needs to be done, we must have a stronger commitment to Christian education—to truly Christian higher education in particular, and especially to Christian *legal* education. It is of the upmost importance to shape the hearts and minds of our young people, to equip them with the right knowledge and the right attitudes. We need to be giving them the tools necessary to build a Christ-centered culture. Allowing young people to fend for themselves with respect to faith, philosophy, and morals has been a slow-moving disaster. We tend to raise our children as believers at home, but then we send them out into the world to institutions that spend their time telling them, "Don't pay any attention to your mom and dad; they don't really know what they are talking about. Don't pay any attention to your pastor; he's just a bigoted puppet of the state. Don't pay any attention to any of those ancient Christians; they were all bad in some way or another. Don't pay any attention to all those former leaders; they all did bad things, so they must be wrong. Instead, pay attention to us."

We need to provide education that teaches truth persuasively instead of just exposing our children to everything everyone believes, or indoctrinating a set of conclusions without reasons. Instead of giving them the biases of the day, we really need to have them delve into what Christians have taught and thought for centuries. It's important to understand Plato and Cicero and other ancients for their insights, their mistakes, and their impact on how we came to be where we are now as a society. Students need to actually investigate what the Bible's implications are, in detail—not just all the milk and bread, but the meat; not just the easy things, but the hard things. We need to talk to them about human nature, the divine order, true wisdom, and making good laws.

Our current educational process has some strong institutions and faculty here and there, but for the most part it is not achieving what needs to be achieved. Today's normal legal education is especially problematic. I heard one professor compare sending someone to secular law school to having someone join a cult. Now, Trinity Law School isn't like that, but most law schools do sort of the same thing the cults do. They put you under tremendous pressure. They assign you thousands of pages to read; you don't really have time to get it all read. They put you under all this pressure emotionally and mentally, and they have you stand up in class and embarrass you with Socratic questions. You relieve that pressure by displaying that you have become a true disciple, that you believe exactly what the law professor seems to want you to believe. The positive part of that, long ago, was that they were really teaching the student the scholastic method—teaching them the way lawyers should think. But the way they're doing it today, there is a subtlety different message.

The secular schools teach instrumentalism, the view that the law is really just a tool to get whatever the client wants. They teach materialism, which is belief that the material world is really all that matters—it's all that is really there, and it is all we really consider when we think about law. They teach positivism, the doctrine that the law is really whatever the government says it is, no matter how contrary to the higher law. They teach a false view of history—or teach no real history at all. Most secular schools do not even teach them the truth about legal history, let alone about Christian history or the history of ideas. They provide a very cynical view of ethics. They think of ethics as based on autonomy and reciprocity—not on right and wrong. They think of ethics as, essentially, giving full disclosure and maintaining the monopoly of the bar association. That isn't what ethics is about. And they teach that power can be used to make words mean whatever you want. Is the public opposed to cloning and the elite all for it? Simply pass a law against cloning, but make it mean something far narrower than the real definition. Then designate the cloning you want to do by a new and unfamiliar scientific name. Do you want a license to do research on humans at an early stage of development? Just redefine what it means to be human.

Instead of letting our children be indoctrinated by the secular law schools without challenge, we really need to teach our students the connection of Christian ideas with the legal system. People need to know the purpose of law and government: to encourage good and restrain evil. They need to know the ideas about human nature and the world, to see it as it really is, all about equity and justice, about God's truth, about when it is appropriate to obey the law, and when it is appropriate to obey God rather than man. They need to know that they need to become people of character, and that being a lawyer is about being a counselor, not just about being a hired gun. Lawyers should not say to their clients, "I know how you can get away with that!" Rather, lawyers should give wise counsel to their clients: "What you want to do, I may be able to provide a defense for you in court when you get sued, but it would be a lot smarter for you not to do that, because people aren't going to like that—it's wrong! A lot of people are going to get hurt and sue you anyway. There are lots of good reasons for you not to do that." Lawyers can be counselors that can discourage people from all sorts of bad conduct. They can be people that can provide advice that improves society instead of driving toward the lowest common denominator.

Talk show host Dennis Prager has observed many times on his radio show that would-be lawyers go into law school thinking morally, but they come out as lawyers who only think about whether actions are arguably legal or not. Now, this transformation from asking if something is wrong to asking if the law will let me get away with it is happening throughout our whole culture. The law is now the actual definition of society's "morality"—if it's legal you can do it; if there is "no controlling legal authority" it's okay; if the authorities cannot put me in jail for it, it must be wholesome. And by manipulating the laws and the legally accepted understanding of words through judicial and political power, people feel they can make anything they want to do "right," and give themselves not only a "right" to do it, but laws to silence their critics as well. Yet, this cultural belief is not really true. And it isn't a particularly good understanding of the law. Law can never overcome the pains of conscience. Law can never justify evil. Human enactments that seek to do so are no longer real laws, let alone the law. The binding force of law comes from the goodness of the law, not the power of the lawmaker.

We need to teach people to be equitable people as well. Aristotle said that equity is not only a kind of justice, but also a virtue. The equitable man doesn't worry about trying to vindicate his own rights all the time. When people do things that hurt him, he forgives them; he is not litigious. On the other hand, the equitable man or woman is zealous for the rights of others. An equitable person acts to protect other people and to make sure that justice is done for his neighbors. We need to become equitable people, and we need to teach our sons and daughters to be equitable people and equitable lawyers.

All of these ideas are part of the vision of Trinity Law School. We think that Christians need to be involved in teaching the truth about these things—instead of just hoping we can go through the world's process, learn everything the way that the relativists see it, and then on the weekend inject a little anti-venom and turn out okay. Instead, it is better to raise people up in the way they should go all along.

CONCLUSION

Ecclesiastes 12:11 says that the words of the wise are like goads. Why does it say that the words are like goads? A goad is a stick that is used to poke an animal to keep it going in the right direction. With the words God gives, he guides us in the right direction. God could have put walls up on both sides of the way so we couldn't get off it. I suppose that for Adam and Eve, before they sinned, it wouldn't have occurred to them to do anything sinful. So, in a sense for them they were on the road and there was a wall on either side until they saw that little gate in the wall that led to the tree of the knowledge of good and evil. But for us, there are no walls. God has given us little pokes with his Word to keep us on the way we should go—Jesus being the way and God's Word being the expression of that way. A poke from a goad is something active; it is not something that is just there. We should be active in reading God's Word and teaching the truth of God's Word to others. In a sense, we participate in that goading. We encourage each other to love and good works. We disciple each other. We teach our children to stay on the path. Christ-centered beliefs, actions, education, and character; all are parts of the goads, the words of the wise in motion. Let us redouble our efforts to heed the words of the wise and pass them on—especially in the areas like human law and government, which, except for issue advocacy, we have often left to other people whose god is made in their own image.

8

Justice in Evangelical Political Theology

Stephen Kennedy

INTRODUCTION

THIS BOOK HAS A place in a larger, ongoing conversation regarding evangelical Christian political involvement since the 1980s. The consequences of that involvement have been, at best, ambiguous. On the one hand, talented Christians with a calling to government service have done wonderful work nationally, locally, and around the world. On the other hand, Christian officeholders and their associates have too often failed to raise the bar of moral accountability or to deepen political discourse. Worst of all, too many of our fellow citizens have developed a negative view of evangelical Christians. If you walk up to someone on the street and ask, "What is a spiritual or a holy person?" she will probably describe someone who is a combination of Mahatma Gandhi and Mother Teresa. Then if you ask, "What about born-again Christians?" she will likely have a negative response. This happens all the time. I see it, and so do you. We blame the press, and some reporters are prosecutorial. However, much of it we've brought down on our own heads. The ambiguous consequences of evangelical political involvement have nothing to do with whether Christians should be politically involved, but rather with how we think about it and how we do it.

The larger matter is that we've failed to communicate a common moral vision in language that ordinary people understand. Ours isn't a failure of style or technique, but rather it's a failure of *thought* and of *character*. It's a failure of thought because the Protestant tradition makes that common vision and language available to us in the larger natural law tradition. It's been there from the beginning, starting with Luther and Calvin who adopted and developed the older tradition, but many have forgotten or rejected it today. It's a failure of character because we've allowed modern and postmodern moral psychology to eclipse our older and better moral psychology of virtues and vices. The language of virtue and vice provided objective language for discussing moral matters in ordinary language. Arguments about *values* are interminable, but if you ask someone what's wise, she will not reply that it's preferable to be a fool!

Natural law is a *recognition*, not a human invention—it reasons that God designed everyone with a capacity to discern the primary contours of the moral universe we inhabit. On one hand, natural law isn't a specifically Christian recognition because it's the moral standard most people around the world and throughout history have lived by, and by which all people will be judged on the last day. On the other hand, natural law recognizes the way God made the world, and Christians have advantages in learning its ways because the Holy Spirit opens the eyes of our hearts to recognize the law of our being, which is clearly displayed in the Bible.

Natural law links human nature to moral action—who we are with what we do. High-medieval and early-Reformation moral psychology understood this relation to be one in which human beings are equipped with the capacity to cultivate virtues, which are cultivated dispositions of the soul. One's character is the sum of virtues and vices resident in the soul at a given moment. Character isn't static, but rather a matter of always becoming either more or less skilled at virtue. For our purposes here, justice and wisdom were thought to be virtues.

The new moral psychology believes that moral action arises from what we feel. The old moral psychology believes that moral action arises from what we practice. Let's make this simple. In the new moral psychology, action is spontaneous. We operate on unstable feelings and sentiments. In this view, we aren't responsible for our emotions. Love, for example, is mostly the rippling tides of how we feel at a given moment. Popular music asks where love is, or whether it's "wild" and "like a heat-wave." Well, if love is like that, it's certainly something you can sell. If love is a series of repeatable emotions and sentiments, then you can sell experiences like that—naturally or perhaps with chemical enhancements. The problem is that this view makes it very difficult to understand how a man or woman sits for long years with a dying spouse patiently, lovingly, and quietly giving encouragement. Virtues are habits. They're habits of the heart. We get good at them by doing them, not by talking. Os Guinness has a wonderful essay entitled, "America's Last Men and Their Magnificent Talking Cure."[1] He argues that we don't become virtuous or really work out our problems by talking; we become skilled at a thing by doing it over and over again. We learn to love by loving. We learn wisdom by practicing wisdom. We learn to be just by doing justice. Virtue is a skill, and it becomes easy, as Dallas Willard said in his chapter earlier, when it's a habit.

In sum, the old moral psychology insists that justice must be practiced and cultivated as a habit in order to excel at it. Evangelicals of the past have been, at times, quite skilled at being just and doing justice, but we have gotten out of the habit. By the time we were aroused from political lethargy we began to talk before we had thought. Without mature habits of justice, we were unwise in many of our pronouncements and activities. We failed to see that natural law and the old moral psychology go hand in glove. Neither one can stand alone. Natural law gives the old moral psychology its appropriate basis for determining laws that make sense for a particular society. The old moral psychology gives natural law the appropriate basis for asserting that virtuous people are capable of making reasonable determinations. You have to believe that people are capable of being wise in order to believe that wisdom is a virtue, and that, as such, it leads to right determinations about how to behave in the world.

David Wells spoke about nature in his chapter. Nature is the realm we can know by reason. God made the world, as the Bible says, according to wisdom. Nature and reason are not abstractions: we can know nature by reason because God made the world according to wisdom and he made us capable of being wise so that we can determine what the world looks like—the moral landscape that determines human flourishing or degradation. Certainly the fall has polluted and corrupted our knowledge of nature and our reasoning capacities. However, a lot of non-Christians are sympathetic to our moral commitments, and a lot of non-Christians are more skilled at virtues than we are. Our theology is often done in ways that can't account for these facts. Evangelical Christians need to be more skilled at politics by making common alliances with people who are sympathetic to our

---

1. In *No God but God*, edited by Os Guinness and John Seel (Chicago: Moody, 1992), 81–94.

moral commitments by using language they understand, and by practicing wisdom, justice, and love.

CREATION AND POLITICAL OBLIGATION

To my mind, evangelical theology has not reckoned well with two key issues since the Reformation: the doctrine of nature, and the proper balance between the individual believer and the organic unity of the church. To these I now turn my discussion.

Creation

The Reformation didn't resolve the ancient church's inadequate doctrine of nature. And when the doctrine of the created-ness of nature was challenged in the nineteenth century, Christians concerned to protect the doctrine of creation from those assaults focused on the mode of creation rather than its implications for life. It was a bold stroke in the wrong direction because Christians reflected less and less on the implications of living in a world that belongs to God, and more and more on possibilities for refuting the scientific assertions of secularists about the world's origins. In other words, we veered toward what the Bible says least about (biochemistry and physics), and ignored what it says most about—the nature of the real world God made and its implications for our lives. (I intend no criticism of those who study and teach about the design of the universe as Christians.)

An inadequate view of nature led to an inadequate view of law. Because we are created by a personal God, and we are made in a particular way—we are *this* and not *that*—some actions cause us to flourish, and other actions bring sadness and disaster to our lives. This idea, revealed clearly in Scripture, concerns what many have called the law of our being, or nature. Law, generally, is concerned with placing fences around human action in order to bring human flourishing and to minimize human suffering. To the extent that law brings human flourishing, it is just; to the extent that it does not, it is unjust. This summarizes Paul's teaching in Romans 13.

The problem with Protestant Christians since the sixteenth century is the way they have understood how the Mosaic law is related to the general purposes of law in a society. Because Saint Paul is so critical of those who want Gentile Christians to come under the authority of Pharisaic

Judaism, they see his criticisms as a carte blanche rejection of law altogether. In this they've failed to understand what law is and does in society. Today, evangelical Christians typically view law as being incapable of doing anything good. They read Paul's insistence that Jewish reliance on the Mosaic law for salvation is useless as meaning that it is useless for people in a modern society to rely on law for an orderly society. Both may be true, but for different reasons. We are utterly and constitutionally incapable of obeying God's law as revealed to Moses, which is why we need redemption in Christ for salvation. However, the moral law revealed to Moses is a law that brings flourishing to individual humans and to human societies, whether people can measure up or not.

Salvation and politics are not the same thing! Politics concerns the legitimate exercise of state power through law. All legitimate state power is concerned with protecting every citizen equally through law, submitting every citizen equally to the law, and securing citizens equally against the bad guys inside and outside the borders—all by laws that should promote virtue and punish vice. Legitimate state power is concerned with justice, peace, and security. That's how we think about law. Law should guarantee that each person remains in possession of what is rightfully hers or his—or, as St. Thomas said, that each receives his due. Well, what is due? What is due is what belongs to each person. Protecting what is ours—and not just personal property, but also the dignity of persons—is the first duty of justice. The law is to guarantee that we remain in possession of what is ours. The problem with having an inadequate account of nature or the law of our nature is that we lose our criteria for knowing what is due to each person.

The second job of justice is to protect that to which we belong. This brings us to the old problem of the importance of human individuality and the organic nature of the church and society. The Reformer's overreaction to Roman Catholic organicism caused an over-emphasis on the individual self and an under-emphasis on human sociality. Protestantism thereby contributed to rise of modernity's "radical individualism." What has been lost is a robust doctrine of God's sociality as well as ours. We affirm the economic necessity of the Trinity without reflecting seriously on God's social nature and our own. Colin Gunton, Oliver O'Donovan, and others have begun wonderfully to develop a more mature doctrine of human sociality in the context of the Trinity, but there's a long way to go, especially in moral and political theology. The importance of our progress in balancing the one and the many is highlighted by the internal tensions of tribalism in traditional societies and the fractured self in postmodern societies—the choice between genocide or suicide.

Justice protects belonging—the things that belong to us, both the properties of our being and our "stuff," on the basis of our sociality, of what we belong to. Injustice, therefore, includes being arbitrarily excluded from those places to which we have rightful belonging. We belong to our families and churches, and as citizens we belong our country. Justice forbids being arbitrarily excluded from these things to which we belong. There are voluntary organizations, like the Rotary and Lions Clubs, or places where we work. But justice must protect against being excluded from those non-voluntary relationships. The clearest example, especially in American society, is the exclusion of minorities.

Exclusion from the full rights of membership is also a loss of belonging. In a fascinating book called *Liberty and Freedom*, David Hackett Fischer points out that there are two traditions in the United States, and one of them died out too quickly. He argues that liberty and freedom were actually two different ideas. Liberty, which is what most of the founders talked about, is derived from the Latin *liber*, and the Greek *eleutheria*, which means to not be impeded, to not have someone telling you what to do all the time. To have liberty is to have freedom of action.

Freedom, on the other hand, has a totally different etymology. It comes from the old Germanic word *frei*, from which we get the words "friend" and "beloved." It means to be a member. If you look at C. S. Lewis's discussion of the word "free" in his book *Studies in Words*, he talks about this and alludes to it as having an antiquated meaning now.[2] This older meaning is no longer really in use because liberty and freedom have been collapsed into synonyms, with both meaning liberty. Very little is said now about membership rights, but those who know that they've been made in the image of a God, who is a social Being, should want very much to protect the rights of membership. It is really the only basis on which to advocate the right of persons not to be excluded from the rights of citizenship on the basis of race, ethnicity, sex, or religion.

So, there are two ways to talk about the things people have that need to be protected. We need protection for our books and household goods, but it is far more important to protect the properties of our being, the

---

2. C. S. Lewis, *Studies in Words* (Cambridge: Cambridge University Press, 1990), 111–32.

properties of our souls and bodies. That we not be tortured, waterboarded, killed, raped, murdered, etc. That our dignity not be assaulted or our reputations be needlessly slandered. There needs to be protections for the things to which we belong. We need not go back and try to change what has happened to the word "freedom." But we must remember that there are membership rights, or rights to the things to which we belong. This is particularly important for peoples in the Two-Thirds World, where belonging is not something that's in a museum—or in a cultural anthropology book—but where it's still a living reality. They know that they belong to their families. We had an African lecturer in Strasbourg a few years ago who said, "In America you have to call and make an appointment with your grandchildren. In Africa, we are always coming." I like that. "We are always coming." In the U.S. we often say to our parents, "Just come over." They say, "We don't want to bother you." In Africa, they don't care! Why? Because they know that they belong to each other.

Some scholars say that there is nothing about human rights in the Bible. I insist that they are wrong. Rights are about belonging—what belongs to us, and what we belong to. A right is a claim of belonging, and the Bible is filled with that language. Indeed, I'm convinced that justice in the Bible is all about belonging—to what and where people belong, and whether they are welcomed and enjoying their rights there. We see this in little, intuitive ways. Our children used to come to us and say, "She took my dress," or "She said I could wear her dress if I let her use my brush, and now she won't let me." What are they complaining about? Something that is theirs has been taken away, or they have not received something that they should have. Or one will say, "Johnny won't let me play," when she shouldn't be excluded at all. If the facts bear out, these little injustices need to be put right so that children learn to be just. Things do belong to us, and we really do belong to things.

Law guarantees belonging. Interestingly, this is precisely what we call a "right." Rights are fundamental to justice, even though they do not exhaust the nature of justice. Rights are not something from the modern age projected onto the Bible. A right is a *claim of belonging*, and belonging is one of the most ancient ideas. We could use other words to represent a claim that something belongs to us, but today we use this word "right." And if a right is a claim of belonging, it is proper to say that God has rights because all things belong to God. Justice requires that we render to God what is his—i.e., our duty (the other fundamental component of justice) is appropriately to honor God's rights through our obedience.

I used to have an old VW camper that was notorious among family and students. The license plate read "SLOOOOW." This thing was a diesel and moved like a tortoise—it fit the license plate! I had every right in the world to blow that thing up with dynamite. It had no claim on me because it's a thing made by human beings. My children have lots of claims on me, but that camper didn't. I could have taken that thing into the desert and blown it up, as long as no one was endangered and I picked up all the litter. I don't owe it anything. I had no duty to that car that I could violate. But you cannot blow up your children. We don't allow that because they have life within them. They are procreated, not made. We beget children, but this book is made. You don't make babies or love—you express love and procreate babies. You make stuff, you don't make humans. In the same way, the Son is eternally begotten of the Father, and the Holy Spirit proceeds from the Father and the Son. God and human beings beget what shares their respective natures. We have duties to what we procreate, not to what we make. God and people have rights, but things do not. People have duties to God and to each other.

The basic human intuition that belonging is the basis of justice is corroborated in the recognition that "the earth is the Lord's." As the creator, God has a right to what he made. In the motif of belonging, the biblical authors recognize God's rightful claims by specifically linking God's creativity with owning the earth. The Bible declares in many ways and passages that *the earth is the Lord's*. It also declares that the earth is the Lord's because he made it. There is a fundamental quality to making that gives rise to a right of belonging. It is not unreasonable, therefore, to say that God has a right to his creation because he made it. The opening verses of Psalm 95, the *Venite*, makes this clear:

> Oh come, let us sing for joy to the LORD,
> Let us shout joyfully to the rock of our salvation.
> Let us come before His presence with thanksgiving,
> Let us shout joyfully to Him with psalms. For the LORD is a great God
> And a great King above all gods,
> In whose hand are the depths of the earth,
> The peaks of the mountains are His also.
> The sea is His, for it was He who made it;

> And His hands formed the dry land.
> Come, let us worship and bow down,
> Let us kneel before the LORD our Maker.
> For He is our God
> And we are the people of His pasture and the sheep of His hand.
>> (vv. 1–7a)

God claims that the earth belongs to him because he made it. If the whole earth belongs to God, can anything belong to us? Yes. We see this as God himself contends for the rights of the poor, the oppressed, and the afflicted. This is probably the most obvious place where we see that God considers the fact that things do belong to people. Ponder these passages:

> For the LORD will plead their case
> And take the life of those who rob them. (Prov 22:23)

> For their Redeemer is strong;
> He will plead their case against you. (Prov 23:11)

> Their Redeemer is strong, the LORD of hosts is His name;
> He will vigorously plead their case
> So that he may bring rest to the earth,
> But turmoil to the inhabitants of Babylon. (Jer 50:34)

> Therefore thus says the LORD,
> "Behold, I am going to plead your case
> And exact full vengeance for you;
> And I will dry up her sea
> And make her fountain dry. (Jer 51:36)

> O Lord, You have pleaded my soul's cause;
> You have redeemed my life. (Lam 3:58)

> I will bear the indignation of the LORD
> Because I have sinned against Him,
> Until he pleads my case and executes justice for me.
> He will bring me out to the light,
> And I will see His righteousness. (Mic 7:9)

There are also passages where God pleads his own case, but in these and many other passages we see that God insists that people's rights be protected, and that he is entirely committed to do so himself. To plead a case is to insist that a right has been violated, as well as a duty abrogated.

The duty is the right of the one violated, but it is also owed to God as the creator of all people.

The proper restraint on what has become, in our time, a problem of rights multiplication—and of rights trivialization—is the fact that the flip side of a right is a duty, and duties are *also* owed to each person. There are properties of our soul, so to speak, which are ours by God's gift. We have rights to these properties, which include the inviolability of our bodies, reputations, etc. But by the exercise of our creativity we also make things, and through various economic means we exchange them for other things we need and want. This *property* also belongs to us, and we own it by right. We have no autonomy in the disposal of this property, and it is ours with some ambiguity, as we see in Leviticus 25, where Moses commands the sabbatical years in which land is to lie fallow (vv. 3–7), and the Year of Jubilee in which every fiftieth year all land was to revert back to the owners who were given specific parcels at the end of the conquest (vv. 8–22)—and finally, summarizing this section, is an astonishing passage in verse 23, "The land, moreover, shall not be sold permanently, for the land is Mine; for you are but aliens and sojourners with Me."

God has rights to call a people for himself, to protect his people, to judge the earth, and to command specific moral laws. Frequently God refers to them as "my judgments" or "my commandments." The possessive pronoun is an indicator of belonging: God's commands and judgments are his by right. He claims the right to command and judge the human inhabitants of the earth, often with the allusion to a court of law before the rest of creation.

Now, are God's rights, and the human rights that are ours by derivation, simply a positivist assertion? Donald McConnell mentioned positivism in his essay, and it means that law is a command. Positivists say that a law is a law as long as it's a command given by a sovereign with a big stick or a gun. Positivism says that law is a command with a sanction. But that's not what we see in Scripture. God's commands make sense according to the kind of beings we are, and according to the kind of world God made. God's commands are communicable to those outside the church because God gives reasons for them. Are God's laws simply demands printed in a book that non-Christians do not believe by a God in whom they do not believe? No, the commandments and judgments of God are made clear in what God has made:

The burden of the word of the LORD concerning Israel. Thus declares the LORD who stretches out the heavens, lays the foundation of the earth, and forms the spirit of man within him, "Behold, I am going to make Jerusalem a cup that causes reeling to all the peoples around; and when the siege is against Jerusalem, it will also be against Judah. (Zech 12:1–2)

He who made the Pleiades and Orion
And changes deep darkness into morning,
Who also darkens day into night,
Who calls for the waters of the sea
And pours them out on the surface of the earth,
The LORD is His name.
It is He who flashes forth with destruction upon the strong,
So that destruction comes upon the fortress. (Amos 5:8–9)

The One who builds His upper chambers in the heavens
And has founded His vaulted dome over the earth,
He who calls for the waters of the sea
And pours them out on the face of the earth,
The LORD is His name..."Behold, the eyes of the Lord GOD are on the sinful kingdom,
And I will destroy it from the face of the earth;
Nevertheless, I will not totally destroy the house of Jacob,"
Declares the LORD. (Amos 9:6, 8)

By the word of the LORD the heavens were made,
And by the breath of His mouth all their host.
He gathers the waters of the sea together as a heap;
He lays up the deeps in storehouses.
Let all the earth fear the LORD;
Let all the inhabitants of the world stand in awe of Him.
For He spoke, and it was done;
He commanded, and it stood fast. (Ps 33:6–9)

For great is the LORD and greatly to be praised;
He is to be feared above all gods.
For all the gods of the peoples are idols,
But the LORD made the heavens.
Splendor and majesty are before Him,
Strength and beauty are in His sanctuary. (Ps 96:4–6)

But when the apostles Barnabas and Paul heard of it, they tore their robes and rushed out into the crowd, crying out and saying, "Men, why are you doing these things? We are also men of the same nature as you, and preach the gospel to you that you should turn from these vain things to a living God, WHO MADE THE HEAVEN AND THE EARTH AND THE SEA AND ALL THAT IS IN THEM." (Acts 14:14–15)

"The God who made the world and all things in it, since He is Lord of heaven and earth, does not dwell in temples made with hands; nor is He served by human hands, as though He needed anything, since He Himself gives to all people life and breath and all things; and He made from one man every nation of mankind to live on all the face of the earth, having determined their appointed times and the boundaries of their habitation, that they would seek God, if perhaps they might grope for Him and find Him, though He is not far from each one of us . . ." (Acts 17:24–27)

. . . in these last days has spoken to us in His Son, whom He appointed heir of all things, through whom also He made the world. And He is the radiance of His glory and the exact representation of His nature, and upholds all things by the word of His power. When He had made purification of sins, He sat down at the right hand of the Majesty on high . . . (Heb 1:2–3)

The natural world itself makes known God's "invisible attributes, His eternal power and divine nature." All of this is made known "through what has been made," according to Romans 1:20–21. We see even more yet in the description of Solomon's wisdom in 1 Kings:

Now God gave Solomon wisdom and very great discernment and breadth of mind, like the sand that is on the seashore. Solomon's wisdom surpassed the wisdom of all the sons of the east and all the wisdom of Egypt. For he was wiser than all men, than Ethan the Ezrahite, Heman, Calcol and Darda, the sons of Mahol; and his fame was known in all the surrounding nations. He also spoke 3,000 proverbs, and his songs were 1,005. He spoke of trees, from the cedar that is in Lebanon even to the hyssop that grows on the wall; he spoke also of animals and birds and creeping things and fish. Men came from all peoples to hear the wisdom of Solomon, from all the kings of the earth who had heard of his wisdom. (4:29–34)

God's commands and judgments aren't from the moon or from Mars. They make sense on the basis of what God has made. Those who understand what's been made should understand how to treat it. This is the very opposite of the so-called naturalistic fallacy. God insists throughout the Bible that he has made the kind of world that makes virtue known to its inhabitants. Further, he insists that we are the kind of creatures that can discern the basic contours of the moral life in the world he made. If we observe carefully what God has made, we see clearly what he requires of us.

This is the reason we begin with the doctrine of creation. God's commands and judgments can be apprehended by reason focused on what has been made—we can know the nature of things as they've been made, and then know what we owe to all things. Human beings can, by reason, recognize in the created order the basic contours of virtue, or godly behavior. Otherwise, they would not justly be held responsible for disobeying it. They do not know it as God's law, but their nature as humans in the wider arena of all nature makes virtue clear to them. We know that this is true because not even in most pop culture do we find songs or art that celebrates hatred, treachery, disloyalty, etc. Go through any music—ancient, high culture, folk, or pop—and I don't think that you will find many songs that celebrate treachery or disloyalty. Most songs lament treachery or disloyalty, indifference, and hatred. People don't sing songs celebrating that their soldiers ran away at the first sight of the enemy, but rather that their army was courageous. Few sing in praise of vice, or to lament virtue.

The fall has polluted and corrupted our reason. But we can still know. We're still held accountable. This doesn't threaten to break out into a good works theology, or Pelagianism. It means that most people have pretty similar moral ideas if they think about it a while, and we can build on those common sympathies in political life. Note that most of the rights guaranteed by international human rights treaties, and embraced around the world, display moral commitments we share with almost everyone who is not in power. Also, focus on the central fact of natural law, as St. Augustine would say: everyone loves something. Or, Bob Dylan: "You're gonna have to serve somebody."

The Trinity and Politics

St. Paul's discussion of the necessity of the state in Romans 13 makes clear that everyone the world over wants legitimate state authority—that is, government that guarantees justice, peace, and security. Even God wants it! Legitimate state authority is not our enemy. The state is for our good, and we are to pay our taxes cheerfully because the state is God's minister of justice! Those with legitimate political authority are servants of God. They merit our respect and support in their difficult vocation. Our exegesis of Romans 13 should point us beyond the state as restraining sin. Paul spends more time in this passage explaining why government is for our good! One finds little basis here for John Locke's doctrine of the "state of nature." It's thoroughly unbiblical.

The doctrine of human sociality is positive—it's derived directly from God's sociality. God is a social being, and so are we. Since we are made in God's image, we are both unique individuals as well as social beings. Adam is a meaningful individual, but he is also made for relationship. In the creation account, God says it is not good for Adam to be alone. God made Adam to be a person in relationship. Alone he's incomplete. Human beings are innately social, as God is social, so Adam needs an *other* with whom to enjoy friendship and intimacy and a family. Adam is made both for the vertical relationship with God, and for the horizontal relationship with fellow human beings.

Why is God not enough for Adam? It's not a sacrilegious question, but rather sensible in the context of the creation account. The clear implication of the text is that by creating Eve, God improves his creation. Indeed, God draws a stark contrast between the previous situation before Eve is created, which was "not good" (Gen 2:18), and the new situation after Eve is created, which is good. It is good that women and men exist. It is important that Adam have someone with whom to share his nature, both for friendship and for fruitfulness. This story reveals that God made us in such a way that we need others to be who God intends us to be. We need others with whom to be in friendship.

Some relations are natural, and others are artificial. Artificial relationships are characterized by the arbitrary nature of their membership. We have no choice but to be members of families and churches. But we can choose to belong to the Rotary Club or the Lion's Club, the Ladies League or the League of Women Voters, the Ford Motor Company or your own business, or the Republican or Democratic parties. Artificial groups are good and necessary things. But our membership in them is arbitrary. There is no moral question over jumping political parties or out of a business corporation.

But the same cannot be said for families and religious organizations. Our individuality is not more important than our sociality. We are not autonomous or self-sufficient. Modern liberalism is founded on the belief that human sociality is the consequence of needing to band together in order to escape what Hobbes called the "state of nature." In Hobbes's theory, we are exclusively individuals, and our sociality is a necessary and negotiated defense against chaos and violence outside civil society—that is, it is the product of artifice. This has become the cornerstone of modern liberal political and jurisprudential theories, but it is not the Christian account of human sociality.

As John Donne wrote, "No man is an island unto himself."[3]

Wendell Berry writes, "Whether we know it or not, whether we want to be or not, we are members of one another . . . The work of the imagination, I feel, is to understand this. I don't think it can be understood by any other faculty."[4]

Individualism as an ideology has led to a destructive quest for human autonomy (literally, "self-law"). It is destructive because it seeks the self-sufficiency possessed only by God as Trinity. The broken, autonomous self needs reintegration back into the lost image of God. The restoration of God's image in us includes the restoration of our personal relationship with God as well as with other people.

The theory of rights that most Westerners are familiar with is derived primarily from the concept of liberty: that justice protects what belongs to us. The theory of rights for groups derives from the idea of freedom. This is not to deny that individuals have membership rights as individuals, or to deny that people in groups have liberty interests. But liberties are usually denied to individuals as individuals, and freedom is usually denied to people in groups due to their belonging to those groups. This would have been helpful during the civil rights movement, I think. Rosa Parks was denied her rights as a citizen because she was an African American, not because she was Rosa. She could get up on the morning and have scrambled eggs instead of cereal, if she wanted to. She could wear a black or a yellow dress, and she could choose between several jobs, I suppose. But one morning she got on a bus, as a tax-paying citizen, and some man got on the bus and said he wanted her seat. "You sit in the back." This was an arbitrary exclusion—a violation of the rights of a citizen—and it was unjust.

3. John Donne, "Meditation XVII."
4. Wendell Berry, *Conversations with Wendell Berry*, edited by Morris Allen Grubbs (Jackson: University Press of Mississippi, 2007), 23.

I come at this problem from my field, international and comparative human rights law. All the international treaties concerning freedom, or membership issues, are designed with this fact in mind: people persecute minorities because of some racial, ethnic, or religious reason. Conversely, people are victims of crimes against humanity, war crimes, gross violations of human rights, torture, or genocide because they are members of racial, ethnic, or religious minorities. Their persecution includes not only the loss of liberties, but also the rights of membership. Justice must guarantee not only against violations of individual liberties, but also against exclusions and oppression based on group identity and belonging.

CONCLUSION

Natural law was lost to Protestants somewhere between Francis Turretin in the late seventeenth century and Charles Hodge in the late nineteenth century. This loss was directly commensurate with another loss: that of a common vision of the moral life under Christ—that is, the church's traditional moral psychology of the virtues. You can't make sense of natural law without the moral psychology that under-girded it for centuries, which recognized the human capacity for virtue. The loss of this moral psychology that gives natural law its plausibility and power was the first to go. By the early twentieth century it gave rise to one of the most unfortunate consequences of fundamentalist anxiety about modernization: the belief that separation from the world entails an inability to share moral concerns with non-Christians. The loss of our old moral psychology, and then of natural law, were complicit in our loss of moral sympathy with non-Christians.

Our chief end as human beings is to become virtuous. Only virtuous men and women can pursue the proper ends of political life. The end of our politics is not merely the maximization of liberties individually and autonomously valued. And the purpose of our economy is not merely the maximization of wealth. Natural law gave way to Locke's doctrine of natural right—the belief that our human *telos* is autonomous liberty, not virtue. This loss meant that natural law as right action came to be thought of as being in conflict with natural right as freedom to pursue one's own conception of the good.

Virtue is the moral psychology that makes sense out of natural law. Without the old view of human beings as capable of cultivating virtues and casting off vice to form mature character, natural law cannot stand. The spiritual disciplines are directed both to deepening our personal relationship to God and to cultivating mature character in the manner I have described. And the doctrine of God's sociality can help us to see that individuals, families, communities, and even nations can be less or more mature in character. A nation that refuses to acknowledge, repent, and make restitution for war crimes, crimes against humanity, and genocide cannot become a mature people. An accurate memory, for example, is necessary for authentic prudence, or practical wisdom.

One problem is that the language we use, even when it involves virtues, is as gaseous as the definitions proffered by secularists—for example, "loving one's neighbor." We've used the words and failed to give them meanings that communicate. Of course, we also fail to compare our definitions to those of others. Then we fail to live them. We fail to insist that love is a skill, not merely an affection.

> "[Politics] represents everything that people do as they live with some intention in community, as they work toward some common purpose, as they carry out responsibilities for the way society develops. Biblically, it is the setting in which God's work with everything and everyone comes to completion (Rev 21). He began his work with a couple in a garden; he completes it with vast multitudes in a city."[5]

Evangelicals' inability to understand the nature of law, of the social dimension of justice, and of true virtue has meant many lost opportunities to have a more profound impact on our society—indeed, on world society. People like Os Guinness, Dallas Willard, and David Wells have been telling us for years that we can't accommodate modernity—or postmodernity—to suit our purposes in the church. It's rife with every destructive solvent the Enlightenment had to offer, in the cultural arena as well as the political and economic arenas. I'm reminded of a story Dallas Willard told about character in an interview with Ken Myers.[6] Dallas was reflecting on the fact that people often say, "This pastor is a really good teacher" or "This pastor is a really good counselor" or "This pastor is a really good administrator." It caused him to ask his wife, "Did the old people

---

5. Eugene H. Peterson, *Where Your Treasure Is: Psalms That Summon You from Self to Community* (Grand Rapids: Eerdmans, 1993) 8–9.

6. Dallas Willard, interview by Ken Myers, *Mars Hill Audio Journal* 36 (January–February 1999).

talk like this when we were young?" Her response was, "The old people used to say, 'He's a good man.'" In all my experience in three seminaries, I remember very little being said about character. Lots of abstract stuff was said about sanctification, but little about mature character. It's this very abstraction that characterizes modernity and the modern church. We need to learn to be skilled in virtues like wisdom, love, and justice.

Restoring natural law and its moral psychology will help us engage our society. Mature character is *not* a commodity. It's *not* the product of a technique. It's *not* a matter of style. It is the result of a long, quiet process of study, thought, contemplation, and prayer. Practical wisdom and justice are virtues necessary for social engagement. But so is love! There are TV ads for a successful dating service where happy folk dance around celebrating the discovery of someone just like them. In modernity, love is a consumable product. You don't get good at it, but rather seek repeatable feelings of connection, sentiment, and affection. Repeatable feelings can be bought and sold. In this manner virtues are commodified. We must show, as Christians, that love is seen in the long, patient skill of a silent lover who waits with his cancer-stricken spouse of fifty years for death to come.

Culture isn't a war zone. It's where family, community, church, education, and the arts remind politicians and businesspersons what's real, true, good, and beautiful. When Ross Perot ran for president, he proclaimed that government should be run like a business. No, it should not. The government is not a business—neither are churches or schools. The government will never be efficient because justice is messy. Governments must be fiscally responsible, but not efficient or profitable. They are different *in kind* from businesses. In the same way that a businessperson would tell a pastor that his business is not an evangelistic association, pastors must resist the techniques and purposes of for-profit corporations. To mingle the two destroys the diversity of concerns that protect the culture from economic necessities.

Conversely, we cannot engage in politics as if the political structure is the church. Politics requires compromise, and the church mustn't ever do that! We should have regarded C. S. Lewis's dire warnings against developing a deep allegiance to any political party.[7] A political party's goal is to gain and to keep power. A Christian's purpose is to grow closer to Jesus

---

7. C. S. Lewis, "Meditations on the Third Commandment," in *God in the Dock: Essays in Theology and Ethics*, edited by Walter Hooper (Grand Rapids: Eerdmans, 1970), 196–99.

Christ and to become virtuous—that is, to cultivate mature, Christlike character. That will mean that a Christian will need to challenge all political parties to be just. We could have avoided being used and abused by political leaders who were indifferent or cynical about our purposes if we'd remembered these important distinctions. Growth in virtue is a long, slow effort of renunciation and celebration involving study, prayer, contemplation, meditation, and the disciplines of the spiritual life brought to bear in order to be skilled at wisdom, justice, and love—to be skilled at obeying Christ.

Contributors

Charles W. Colson—a popular author, speaker, and radio commentator. A former presidential aide to Richard Nixon and founder of Prison Fellowship, he has written several books, most recently *God and Government* and *The Faith*. In 1993 Colson was awarded the prestigious Templeton Prize for Progress in Religion, given for extraordinary leadership and originality in advancing humanity's understanding of God.

Os Guinness—author and social critic, has written or edited more than twenty-five books, including *The Call, Long Journey Home, Unspeakable*, and *The American Hour*. A frequent speaker and seminar leader at political and business conferences in the United States, Europe, and Asia, Guinness has also lectured at many of the world's leading universities and has often spoken on Capitol Hill. He lives in Washington, DC.

Stephen Kennedy—an associate professor at Trinity Graduate School at the Santa Ana, California campus. He teaches courses on Communication and Culture as well as International and Comparative Human Rights Law and International Humanitarian Law (the law of war). His current research includes the theology of human rights, the protection of religious liberties—especially those of Native Americans and indigenous peoples, and the problems associated with terrorist violence and religious liberties protection. For the past eight years, Professor Kennedy has been the director of Trinity's European program in Strasbourg, France, leading students to the International Institute of Human Rights.

Vishal Mangalwadi—described by *Christianity Today* as "India's foremost Christian intellectual," is an international lecturer, social reformer, political columnist, and author of fourteen books. Born and raised in India, he studied philosophy at universities, in Hindu *ashrams*, and at L'Abri Fellowship in Switzerland. In 1976 he turned down several job offers in the West to return to India, where he and his wife, Ruth, founded a community to serve the rural poor. It was Mangalwadi's books *When the New Age Gets Old* and *India: The Grand Experiment* that first brought his works to the attention of the American public. In demand worldwide, Vishal is a dynamic, engaging speaker who has lectured in thirty-two countries. He enjoys simplifying complex ideas and inspiring despairing hearts with hope. Along with some friends, Vishal is pioneering Rivendell Sanctuary—a new kind of college restoring sacredness to higher education.

Paul A. Marshall—Senior Fellow at the Hudson Institute's Center for Religious Freedom. He has testified many times before Congress, lectured at the U.S. Department of State, the U.S. Helsinki Commission, and the asylum bureaus of the INS, and spoken on human rights at the Chinese Academy of Social Sciences in Beijing. He is the author of over twenty books, including the best-selling, award-winning survey of religious persecution worldwide entitled *Their Blood Cries Out*, and more recently, *God and the Constitution*.

Donald McConnell—dean of Trinity Law School at the Santa Ana, California, campus of Trinity International University. He earned a BA in 1982 from Westmont College and a JD in 1985 from the University of Southern California. Admitted to the California Bar in 1985, he practiced law between 1985 and 2001 in the areas of maritime tort litigation, insurance defense litigations, products liability law, and real estate litigation, among others. After many semesters of teaching as an adjunct for Trinity Law School and its predecessor, Simon Greenleaf School of Law, between 1988 and 2001, he became a full-time faculty member at Trinity in 2001. He has participated in over twenty hours of radio interviews and discussions, given over two dozen lectures at various locations outside the school, and authored the essay "Why Natural Law Is Called Natural" for the 2008 symposium issue of the *Liberty Law Review*. He also posts to a blog at http://trinitariandon.blogspot.com.

Patrick Nolan—president of Justice Fellowship, the criminal justice reform division of Prison Fellowship Ministries. Justice Fellowship works to reform the criminal justice system based on the principles of restorative justice found in the Bible. He served for fifteen years in the California State Assembly, four of those as Assembly Republican Leader. He was a leader on crime issues, particularly on behalf of victims' rights.

Contributors

Roger N. Overton—currently pursuing a master's degree at Talbot School of Theology. He has addressed various churches, schools, and youth camps throughout the United States. Roger was coeditor of *The New Media Frontier* and currently blogs at http://ateamblog.com.

David F. Wells—BD (University of London), ThM (Trinity Evangelical Divinity School); PhD (Manchester University), post-doctoral research fellow (Yale Divinity School), is Distinguished Research Professor at Gordon-Conwell Theological Seminary and an ordained Congregational minister. He has authored or edited sixteen books, including *Above All Earthly Pow'rs* and *Losing Our Virtue*. He and his wife, Jane, live in South Hamilton, Massachusetts.

Dallas Willard—professor in the School of Philosophy at the University of Southern California. His philosophical publications are mainly in the areas of epistemology, the philosophy of mind and of logic, and the philosophy of Edmund Husserl. He also lectures and publishes in religion. *Renovation of the Heart* (2002) received *Christianity Today*'s 2003 Book Award in the category of spirituality, and *The Divine Conspiracy* (1998) was selected as *Christianity Today*'s Book of the Year for 1999.

www.ingramcontent.com/pod-product-compliance
Lightning Source LLC
Chambersburg PA
CBHW070918160426
43193CB00011B/1516